Study Philippians: 8 Practical Lessons On Joyfully Living For Christ

Jason Dexter

Author and General Editor

Study Philippians: 8 Practical Lessons on Joyfully Living for Christ
Copyright © 2023 by Jason Dexter

D0113196

Study and Obey

TABLE OF CONTENTS

Philippians 1:1-18

Outline

I. Greetings (1-2)
II. Paul prays joyfully for the Philippians' growth (3-11)
III. Paul's imprisonment resulted in the spread of the gospel (12-18)

I. Greetings (1-2)

Discussion Questions

- Where was Paul when he wrote this book?
- Who was the audience?
- Where was Philippi? (Macedonia, named after the father of Alexander the Great)
- Which Bible passage tells about Paul's original journey to Philippi? (Acts 16)
- What major events happened to Paul there? (Cast demon out of slave girl, was thrown into prison and an earthquake in the middle of the night opened the gates and knocked off their chains. A jailer and his family came to know Christ.)
- Who is Timothy?

Cross-References

Acts 16 - Background for the Epistle to the Philippians. This chapter tells about Paul's mission efforts in Philippi.

Teaching Points

1. Philippians is another of the prison epistles. These were written during Paul's imprisonment in Rome. Numerous references are made to his imprisonment, as well as the praetorian guard (1:13). Paul actually carried on an active ministry during his incarceration. He shared with many guards and even part of Caesar's own household (Philippians 4:22.) Likely, Paul was not in a dungeon or high-security prison. The circumstances described sound more like house arrest. We know his friends had some freedom to come and go, just like Onesimus in Philemon.

2. Paul originally visited Philippi on his second missionary journey. Lydia was one of the saints there. A demon-possessed slave girl followed Paul around for several days, leading to him getting irritated and casting the demon out. Paul's casting out of the demon caused a big ruckus among the people, and the owners of this fortune teller had Paul and Silas thrown into prison. In the middle of the night, as they were singing praise songs, there was an earthquake. Their chains fell off, and the doors opened. Paul later shared with the jailer, who was saved along with his household. Subsequently, the city leaders wanted Paul to leave secretly once they realized he was a Roman and they were illegally imprisoning him. He refused, demanding that they come to him publicly (Acts 16:35-40.)

3. Philippians was a Roman colony and immensely proud of its Roman citizenship. Although located in Greece, its government was modeled after Italian towns. Apparently, Timothy was with Paul at the time of this writing.

4. The tone of Paul's letter to the Philippians is exceedingly positive, perhaps the most positive out of all his epistles. He mentions very few negative things about them. They are a church that is doing well, unlike the Corinthians, who were rife with problems and strongly rebuked by Paul.

But, although they were doing well, Paul did not ignore them or assume they would continue to do well. He still wrote, encouraging them to keep pressing on to even greater heights.

Application: We can learn from this that it is important not to grow complacent with our spiritual level or with the spiritual level of those we teach. Doing well yesterday does not guarantee we will do well today. Growth requires perseverance and dedication.

II. Paul prays joyfully for the Philippians growth (3-11)

Discussion Questions

- How would you describe the tone of Paul's letter? (1:3-12)
- How would you describe Paul's relationship with the Philippians?
- How did Paul feel about them?
- What positive things does he mention about them?
- What negative things does he mention about them?
- Since he can't meet them face to face, what does he do instead?
- What two qualities can you see in Paul's prayer (thanks and joy)?
- What can we learn from this?
- What is the main content of Paul's prayer? What can we learn from this?
- Can you see any strength of the Philippians? What does Paul pray in regard to the areas they are already strong?

Cross-References

John 10:27-30 - My sheep listen to my voice; I know them, and they follow me. I give them eternal life, and they shall never perish; no one will snatch them out of my hand. My Father, who has given them to me, is greater than all[a]; no one can snatch them out of my Father's hand. I and the Father are one.

Ephesians 1:13-14 – And you also were included in Christ when you heard the message of truth, the gospel of your salvation. When you believed, you were marked in him with a seal, the promised Holy Spirit, who is a deposit guaranteeing our inheritance until the redemption of those who are God's possession—to the praise of his glory.

2 Cor 5:10 – For we must all appear before the judgment seat of Christ, so that each of us may receive what is due us for the things done while in the body, whether good or bad.

1 Peter 1:22 – Now that you have purified yourselves by obeying the truth so that you have sincere love for each other, love one another deeply, from the heart.

2 Corinthians 1:12 – Now this is our boast: Our conscience testifies that we have conducted ourselves in the world, and especially in our relations with you, with integrity and godly sincerity. We have done so, relying not on worldly wisdom but on God's grace.

Philippians 2:15 – So that you may become blameless and pure, "children of God without fault in a warped and crooked generation." Then you will shine among them like stars in the sky.

Teaching Points

1. Paul may not have been able to do the kind of ministry he had done before with a lot of traveling and church planting, but he didn't allow this to discourage or keep him from the work. Where there is a will, there is a way. Paul had the will to do ministry, no matter the circumstances, so he found a way. Though he wasn't free to go where he may have wanted, Paul could share with the people around him, and he did. Besides that, he wrote letters to the people he couldn't visit while praying for them often.

Application: We should not make excuses for not reaching out to others. Paul could have become focused on himself and his own problems. It would have been natural for him to expect others to care for and pray for him. He could have looked back on his long ministry and rested on his laurels. But he didn't. Even in prison, he sought ways to reach out. Sickness, disability, persecution, age, gender--none of these are reasons to stop doing the ministry God has called us to. Serving God despite many difficulties and challenges is also a great inspiration to others.

2. If we have the desire to share the gospel, there is always an opportunity to do so. If you can't speak, you can write. If you are blind, you can still talk. If you are on a plane, you can share with the person next to you. If you are in the park, you can share with lonely elderly people. If your parents don't want to see you, you can write. People have numerous excuses for not sharing the good news. Here are a few of them:

- I don't know enough.
- I am not good enough.
- They will not listen to me.
- I am busy. I will do it later.
- I don't have many opportunities.
- I am scared/nervous.

Paul had a good "reason," too, for not sharing the gospel. He was wrongfully imprisoned. But that didn't stop Paul. We would do well to remember Paul's statement in Romans 1:16, "I am not ashamed of the gospel of Christ, for it is the power of God."

In Exodus 3, Moses made many of these same excuses. And to every one of them, God replied, "I will be with you." God will be with you. His Word is powerful. Open your mouth and "tell of his deeds in songs of joy." (Psalm 107:22)

2. As we see in all the books Paul writes, he actively prays for those he ministers to. In almost every one of his letters, it is evident that he consistently prays for those in his ministry. It is important for us to follow his example in continually praying for those we reach out to, whether they are our children, students, Bible study members, or disciples.

Why was Paul's ministry so effective? Was it his method? Probably partly. Was it his education level? That likely didn't hurt. Was it God's blessing? Definitely.

But why did God bless him? Paul was a man of prayer. God used his prayer to accomplish great things. So I ask, do you pray regularly for the people you share with, for your co-workers, your family, friends, and brothers and sisters in Christ?

What can we learn from Paul's prayer?

A. He didn't take God's answers for granted. Paul prayed with thanksgiving. He realized it was God's work in the Philippians' lives, and he was grateful for that work (Philippians 1:6). When God blessed Paul's ministry, he thanked Him for it. We should do the same.

B. He was joyful. Paul's joy signified that he cared deeply for the Philippians. Ministering to them wasn't just a job, a routine to him. Paul loved them like a father and a close friend. Their successes excited him. At the same time, their failures concerned him.

C. He prayed for spiritual growth. Look at the actual requests Paul makes to the Lord on their behalf. What are they? He prays for their love to abound more and more, for their knowledge and discernment. Paul prays that they will approve the things which are excellent and that they will live with sincerity and blamelessness. You don't see him praying for their careers, health, long life, or exams. Not that he never prayed for these things (in James, we are commanded to pray for the sick), but he realized these were not the most important issues.

Application: What is the main content of your prayer life? For many people, prayers are often shallow and focused on our temporal and physical needs. We learn from Paul and other great men and women of prayer to go deeper. Paul's prayers focus on the most critical things: character and spiritual growth. By all means, continue praying for the sick, the weak, and the poor. Pray for health, strength, and provision. But go beyond this. Plead with God for character growth. Ask God to turn weaknesses into strengths. Identify areas of shortcoming, and pray for change in those areas. Spend some time evaluating the type of things you normally pray for. And make sure that your prayers reflect God's heart, not your own.

D. He prayed that their strengths would become even stronger. In other words, Paul wasn't content that they were doing well. He wanted them to reach onward and upward.

Application: No matter how good we are at something, there is always room for growth. No one is perfect, not even in a single area. Do not become complacent. And that is the theme of Philippians: press on. Press on toward the prize (Philippians 3:14).

3. We also see Paul's deep care and close bond with the Philippians in this passage. Their relationship gives us a good example of the kind of fellowship we should have with others. The Philippians were Paul's spiritual children, but they still were able to encourage Paul through their willingness to put into practice what he taught and their co-participation in the gospel.

Application: Whether you are a new believer or a teacher of many years, you can have solid fellowship with others. Come alongside your brothers and sisters in Christ, work together and strengthen each other. Do not think that you have little to offer just because you are a new believer. God gifts every believer with exactly what they need to build His kingdom, how He wants and when He wants.

4. Paul is very God focused. He is keenly aware that it is God's grace working in them, and through him.

Philippians 1:6 - *Being confident of this, that he who began a good work in you will carry it on to completion until the day of Christ Jesus.*

Their good qualities were all the result of God's work in their lives. Paul knew that God would finish this work in them that He began. This shows our salvation is God's initiative. He is the beginning and the end, the source and finisher of our spiritual life. This gives us eternal security and the confidence to know that God will never forsake or abandon us. Because sanctification is God's work in our lives, we can be confident it will be carried on to completion.

III. Paul's imprisonment resulted in the spread of the gospel (12-18)

Discussion Questions

- How would you describe Paul's reaction to his imprisonment?
- What attitude did he have?
- How did his unfair imprisonment affect his demeanor?
- How do you think the Philippians might have felt about Paul's imprisonment?
- What did Paul say to encourage them?
- How did God use Paul's imprisonment to work together for good?
- How can we remember this principle when we face difficulties in our own lives?
- How can we use our own troubles to encourage other believers?
- In what two ways was the gospel being spread?
- What selfish motivation could possibly push someone to share the gospel?
- What are Paul's thoughts about this?
- What should be your motive for sharing the gospel?

Cross-References

Ephesians 4:29 - Do not let any unwholesome talk come out of your mouths, but only what is helpful for building others up according to their needs, that it may benefit those who listen.

James 5:9 - Don't grumble against one another, brothers and sisters, or you will be judged. The Judge is standing at the door!

1 Corinthians 10:10 – And do not grumble, as some of them did—and were killed by the destroying angel.

Proverbs 15:13 - A happy heart makes the face cheerful, but heartache crushes the spirit.

Proverbs 17:22 – A cheerful heart is good medicine, but a crushed spirit dries up the bones.

Teaching Points

1. Paul practiced what he preached. He often taught others to be joyful, not to complain, to trust God in every circumstance, and to realize that God is sovereign over everything.

Romans 8:28 - *And we know that in all things God works for the good of those who love him, who have been called according to his purpose.*

1 Thessalonians 5:18 - *Give thanks in all circumstances; for this is God's will for you in Christ Jesus.*

He didn't just say that because it was always others who were in trouble and never himself. Paul faced many more hardships than the average share. Yet he never complained. He was joyful in the Philippi prison, and now he continued to be joyful while imprisoned in Rome.

Why could he have such a positive attitude?

His chief goal was for the gospel to be spread, and he recognized that this situation afforded many unique opportunities to disseminate the gospel. We should learn from Paul and always look for the silver lining in our own circumstances.

Application: Don't focus on the negative things or become a complainer. If you complain, against whom are you complaining? If I complain about the cold and wet weather, I am complaining against God. If I complain that my baby wakes up in the middle of the night, I am also complaining against God, who allowed this to happen, perhaps to build up my patience and compassion. God has a reason for everything. Can you share an example of something difficult that happened in your life that God used for good?

2. What concrete benefits were there for Paul being imprisoned?
- More time for prayer.
- More time for writing epistles.
- A testimony that others could look to so that they might become bold in their own sharing. We have modern-day examples of this as well. After Jim Elliot and his friends gave their lives to reach the Quechua Indians, it sparked a movement of missionaries around the world. This is one reason we must always be joyful and take advantage of the opportunities we have. Our reactions can influence others as well.
- Opportunities to share with people who would have been particularly hard to share with in normal circumstances, such as his prison mates, guards, and perhaps even Nero (we don't have any direct evidence of it, but knowing Paul's personality, it is very likely he shared with Nero during his appeal).
- More time for meditation in his own walk with the Lord.
- More responsibility for his co-workers, e.g., Timothy and Titus.

3. Some people were motivated positively by Paul's imprisonment to share the gospel, but others were motivated by selfish incentives.

What possible selfish reasons could motivate someone to share the gospel?

Here are a few possibilities:

- Quest for personal recognition
- Popularity among the saints
- A feeling of power
- Earning favor with God
- Financial gain

While Paul didn't agree with their motivations, he was happy that the gospel was going forth and that through their preaching people could be saved. God looks at the heart and would not reward someone with wrong motivations since they already have received their reward (respect of men) in full. But as long as the message was true, then people could hear it and have the opportunity to be saved.

For us, we should examine ourselves and make sure we have the right basis for sharing the gospel. What is the right reason? Love.

Application: Are you regularly sharing the gospel? When was the last time you shared with someone? Spend a few minutes thinking about who in your circle you could pray for. Write down 3-5 names. Are you willing to commit to pray for these people regularly? Can you make an appointment with one of them this week to share with them about Christ?

Philippians 1:19-30

Outline

I. Paul expected to be delivered one way or another from his bondage (19-20)
II. To live is Christ and to die is gain (21-26)
III. Live worthily of the gospel and of suffering (27-30)

I. Paul expected to be delivered one way or another from his bondage (19-20)

Discussion Questions

- What is Paul referring to in verse 19?
- What possible way, or ways, could he be delivered? Was he delivered?
- What do the words "earnest expectation" indicate about Paul's attitude toward the future?
- What might our attitude be in a similar position?
- Was Paul bold? How? How could Paul's death glorify God?
- Can you truthfully say Christ is always exalted in your body?
- What is one thing you can do with your body to exalt Christ?

Cross-References

Romans 12:12 – Be joyful in hope, patient in affliction, faithful in prayer.

Galatians 4:6 – Because you are his sons, God sent the Spirit of his Son into our hearts, the Spirit who calls out, "Abba, Father."

Acts 28:30 – For two whole years Paul stayed there in his own rented house and welcomed all who came to see him.

1 Timothy, 2nd Timothy, Titus – The events in these letters can't be harmonized with the book of Acts, leading scholars to believe Paul was released the first time (as he expected) from Rome and did further ministry before being imprisoned again several years later.

Matthew 10:32 – Whoever acknowledges me before others, I will also acknowledge before my Father in heaven.

Titus 2:8 – And soundness of speech that cannot be condemned, so that those who oppose you may be ashamed because they have nothing bad to say about us.

1 Peter 3:16-17 – Keeping a clear conscience, so that those who speak maliciously against your good behavior in Christ may be ashamed of their slander. For it is better, if it is God's will, to suffer for doing good than for doing evil.

Colossians 3:17 – And whatever you do, whether in word or deed, do it all in the name of the Lord Jesus, giving thanks to God the Father through him.

Teaching Points

1. Philippians is a book filled with practical points on Christian living. Many of these practical applications for Christian living come directly from the life of Paul. He imparts many of his own experiences with the Philippians, what God is doing in the middle of these experiences, and how God is using them in his life and for the kingdom.

The church was doing exceptionally well, so apparently the Philippians didn't have a lot of need for being retaught the foundation of the gospel or basic doctrines. Unlike the Galatian church, they were not being infiltrated with heretical teachers. But they did have a close connection to Paul and would have wanted to know how his imprisonment could be part of God's plan and what Paul thought of it.

Below are the main themes of the chapter, and we will discuss many of these subsequently.

- Paul's expectation of deliverance.
- Paul's desire to be a good testimony in the middle of this trial.
- Paul's resolution to live for the Lord while he could.
- Paul's hope for being with Christ.
- Paul's realization that staying on earth to share the gospel for a while was still necessary.
- Paul's exhortation to live worthily of the gospel.
- Paul's declaration that they would also face suffering for the sake of the gospel.

2. Paul's expectation of deliverance (verses 19-25)

Paul was at a crossroads. It is evident that he anticipated some kind of decision regarding his imprisonment in the near future. He realized it could be a death sentence (he talks of death several times), yet he expressed the belief and the hope that he would be delivered soon. This expectation was not stated as a prophecy or a revelation from the Lord.

Rather, it would have been Paul examining the facts of the case and disposition of whoever was the judge, combined with the belief that his ministry was not yet over. We can see from verse 19 that he placed his faith in God, recognizing the importance of the Philippians' prayers and the Spirit's provision. If God wanted him to be delivered, then he would be delivered.

We should make a note here that the book of Acts ends with Paul under house arrest in Rome and tells us that he was there for two years (Acts 28:17-31.) There is no further narrative account of what happened to Paul after that. This ending has led to several theories. We can only glean some historical data from this book and others.

The main consensus among scholars is that Paul was, in fact, freed for

16

several years after this two-year house arrest period. The main reasons for this are found in the books of 1 Timothy, 2nd Timothy, and Titus. In these accounts, Paul describes some of his travels, yet these travels are not expressed in the book of Acts.

The conclusion is that Paul went on more journeys in addition to the three recorded in Acts. For this to happen, Paul would have to have been released and then later arrested and beheaded, as tradition teaches us. This would also fit with these verses which show that Paul fully expected to be released soon.

Whether or not he was finally released for a period of time, we can see Paul's dependence on the Lord and his optimistic attitude even amid challenging circumstances.

2. Paul desired to be a good testimony in the middle of this trial (20) -

We do see Paul show some concern in his imprisonment. What is his concern? It is not fear or worry for his future or his physical well-being. He is instead concerned that his testimony will suffer and that he will not bring glory to Christ. The very fact that this is Paul's concern shows us his inner priorities.

Are most prisoners primarily concerned with being a good testimony to their fellow prisoners? Of course not! They are focused on getting out!

If Paul did have to face death and, in fear for his life, renounced Christ, made excuses for his behavior, or tried to backpedal, it would put him to shame and not exalt Christ. He wanted to be bold. Whatever would happen, Paul was resolved to exalt Christ first and foremost with his actions and words. To him, this was far more important than even life or death.

Application: We should look at our own lives and the trials that we go through. Then we should consider our own attitudes. Are we scared of making a stand for God? Are we more worried about money or materials than about exalting the Lord? If Christ were sitting next to us, would He be ashamed of us? Would we be ashamed knowing He is watching?

Following is the story of a martyr, Felix Manz, and his friends who boldly stood for Christ and showed no shame but testified to the Lord until their deaths.

In 1525 Zwingli and Manz split over the issue of infant baptism. Felix felt it was a compromise with the papists (the Roman Catholics). The city council sided with Ulrich Zwingli. Felix Manz and his friends (among them Conrad Grebel and Georg Blaurock) were ordered to recant and have their infants baptized.

Not only did Manz and friends refuse, but they immediately held a meeting and conducted adult baptisms, a crime the Zurich city council made punishable by drowning within two months.

Felix Manz would prove the first victim of the wrath of the city council and Ulrich Zwingli. On January 5, 1527, Felix was led from prison to a boat. On the way, he praised God and preached to the people gathered to watch him die.

One of Zwingli's priests went along, still trying to convert him. Manz's brother and mother were there as well, urging him to stand fast.

He was put into a boat on the river Lammat. His hands were tied, and he was made to squat down. A stick was stuck behind his knees and above his elbows to immobilize him, and he was taken to the middle of the river.

There, with his mother, brother, and his fellow "rebaptizers" (Anabaptists) shouting encouragement, he was tipped into the lake, a final death by baptism.

He was not horrified nor afraid. His last words were, "Into your hands, O Lord, I commend my spirit."

II. To live is Christ and to die is gain (21-26)

Discussion Questions

- What does it mean "to live is Christ"?
- Where does the world find meaning in life?
- What were the advantages of each of the possible roads (death and life) in front of him?
- Is verse 25 a supernatural revelation or just a firm belief on Paul's part?
- Is there anything in this world holding you back from wanting to be with Christ in heaven?
- Is there anything in this world that makes you hope that Jesus will come back later to give you more time on earth?
- Are you scared of dying, or do you have the same calm assurance that Paul had that dying is immensely beneficial?
- If you were in Paul's position of being wrongfully imprisoned, what kind of things would you write to your family/friends/brothers/sisters in Christ?

Cross-References

2 Corinthians 5:8 – We are confident, I say, and would prefer to be away from the body and at home with the Lord.

Galatians 2:18-20 – If I rebuild what I destroyed, then I really would be a lawbreaker.
"For through the law I died to the law so that I might live for God. I have been crucified with Christ and I no longer live, but Christ lives in me. The life I now live in the body, I live by faith in the Son of God, who loved me and gave himself for me.

1 Peter 5:10 - And after you have suffered a little while, the God of all grace, who has called you to his eternal glory in Christ, will himself restore, confirm,

strengthen, and establish you.

Romans 8:18 - For I consider that the sufferings of this present time are not worth comparing with the glory that is to be revealed to us.

1 Thessalonians 2:11-12 – For you know that we dealt with each of you as a father deals with his own children, encouraging, comforting and urging you to live lives worthy of God, who calls you into his kingdom and glory.

Teaching Points

1. Paul's resolve to live for the Lord while he could. 21-24

John 9:4 - *As long as it is day, we must do the works of him who sent me. Night is coming, when no one can work.*

Paul didn't know when the end of his life would be. It could be very soon. This knowledge made him all the more resolved to make use of each minute, to serve the Lord with every last remaining opportunity. He would not be one of the saints who, on his deathbed, regretted spending too little time sharing the Word and too much time engrossed in the world. Galatians 2:18-20

He was so focused on Christ that he even said, "to live is Christ." It was, in effect, Christ living in and through Paul, since he was subordinating his own sinful desires to the will of God.

Application: Are we about "me," or are we about "Christ"? Are we taking advantage of the opportunities that we have? None of us seem to be approaching that stretch of the end of our life like Paul appeared to be. Not prioritizing Christ could make us put off wholeheartedly serving the Lord until some unknown future point. How many of us have thought to ourselves we will do this or that for the Lord later when we have more time?

I know I have thought this myself. Perhaps sometime later, when I can be in full-time ministry, I will have more energy or time for sharing the Word.

Perhaps later, when the moment is just right, I will share with some of my co-workers I haven't shared with yet. Well, that future time may never arrive. One of Satan's most effective temptations is to tell believers, "Yes, you should do that good work for God. Just do it... later."

So, what should we do? Resolve to live for the Lord while we can. This starts with your own walk with the Lord, then extends to your family, church, and ministry.

2. Paul's hope for being with Christ -

As much as Paul did take advantage of every opportunity for serving the Lord, he had an even greater desire. What was that? His desire was to be with Christ. Going home to be with the Lord was Paul's greatest hope, his greatest joy. His death would finally mark the finish line of his race on earth, and the beginning of a brand-new life, in heaven with the Lord.

Paul wasn't attached to this world. He didn't want to hold off death for any selfish motivations. He didn't have any more worldly goals he wanted to achieve first before he was ready. He was prepared to go then and there. Although he was ready, that didn't mean he wasted his time until actually going to be with Christ. He didn't sit around dreaming of heaven and doing nothing on earth. His hope to be with Christ further motivated him to spread the gospel. Why? He wanted others to also have this same chance and this same hope to be with Christ themselves.

Notice also that the text doesn't say he wanted to depart to go to heaven. In fact, it doesn't even mention heaven or paradise. Sometimes when sharing the gospel, a preacher will ask, "Do you want to go to heaven?" Someone may eagerly respond yes. But a better question is, "Do you want to be with Christ?" Paul is excited not about heaven but about the opportunity to be with Christ!

Bringing it home: Would you want to go to heaven if Christ wasn't there? Would you be happy that you could still leave the pain and turmoil of this earth behind and not have God always "looking over your shoulder"? Or would you arrive in heaven and feel disappointed/crushed to discover that despite so much gold, heavenly food, perfect music, no crying, no tears, and perfect health, etc., God was not there?

Hopefully, we do hope to be with the Lord, and hopefully, this is centered on wanting to be *with Him*.

III. Live worthily of the gospel and of suffering (27-30)

Discussion Questions

- Does verse 27 teach that we can ever be worthy of salvation? Then what does it mean?
- Are you living worthy of the gospel?
- What word sums up Paul's desire for them in the second part of verse 17?
- What does verse 28 mean?
- How would their calm/bold response to their opponents signal their opponents' destruction?
- What does the word "granted" mean?
- Do you think of suffering for Christ as a gift? Is it a gift? Why?
- In what way might the Philippians have suffered for Christ?
- Share about a time you have suffered for Christ. How was your response? How should you respond?

Teaching Points

1. Paul realized that staying on earth to share the gospel for a while was still necessary.

Although Paul wanted to be with Christ, he realized his job was not quite finished yet. Again, this shows Paul's unselfish nature (which, in fact, he teaches about in the very next chapter). Even though he would personally want to be with God sooner, there was more to consider than only himself. Many people could still benefit greatly from his teaching and, to some extent, still needed him.

2. Paul's exhortation to live worthily of the gospel.

Similar exhortations are found throughout Paul's epistles. In no way does this mean that we can ever earn or deserve salvation. Of course, that is impossible. Instead, Paul is teaching that the gospel should motivate us to godly living. It should invoke a response where we desire to live our lives up to God's standards, not to earn salvation, but simply to please God, who gave so much for us.

1 John 4:19 - *We love because He first loved us.*

This is yet another reminder that the gospel is not just to give us head knowledge. It is supposed to change our behavior.

Beyond this, we see Paul exhorting the Philippians to be unified.

Philippians 1:27b - *I will hear of you that you are standing firm in one spirit, with one mind striving together for the faith of the gospel.*

His absence would leave a void where it would be easier for false leaders to enter or divisions to rise up. This is generally the case when a strong and mature authority leaves a church. Paul did not want this to happen to them. He desired unity. This is reminiscent of Jesus' high priestly prayer in John, where he prays for unity for the disciples after His absence. Seeing it taught so much should remind us that unity is essential. We should stand firm together with one spirit and one mind pushing one another forward towards God and spreading the Word.

3. Paul's declaration that they would also face suffering for the sake of the gospel.

In the past, I have been guilty of taking this verse out of context (because I memorized it from a card) and concluding that all believers are guaranteed to face suffering/persecution. Actually, Paul is teaching that the Philippians will face suffering, not necessarily everyone.

However, it is a reasonable assumption that since the world is still anti-Christ, many believers today who take a stand for Christ will still face varying degrees of suffering and persecution, though likely not to the degree of the early New Testament saints.

Paul uses the word "granted," which is similar to the word "given." It is almost as if it is a favor, a privilege. Indeed, it is a privilege to suffer for Christ. Do you think so? Why?

The verse shows that believers should expect to suffer. If we expect it, it will help us to prepare mentally and spiritually and to commit ahead of time to standing firm in the face of pressure. When we do face troubles for Christ, we should thank God that we are worthy to suffer for Him. And we should make sure that the reason we are suffering is the right reason and that we respond to it correctly, being a good testimony for Him.

1 Peter 3:17 - *For it is better to suffer for doing good, if that should be God's will, than for doing evil.*

Philippians 2:1-11

Outline

I. Paul's exhortation to unity and unselfishness (1-5)
II. Christological doctrinal passage on the incarnation of Christ (6-8)
III. Christological doctrinal passage on the exaltation of Christ (9-11)

I. Paul's exhortation to unity and unselfishness (1-5)

Discussion Questions

- Why does Paul make so many "if" statements in verse 1?
- Knowing that these things are true, what response does Paul hope they will evoke in the Philippians?
- What gave Paul joy? What gives you joy?
- What is a summary of his goal for them in verse 2?
- How do divisions affect a church? Its effectiveness? Its testimony? Its growth?
- When does Paul say it is allowed to be selfish?
- How would you define selfishness?
- Share an example of an area you are tempted to be selfish.
- What does the term "empty conceit" mean?
- Why should we consider others as more important than ourselves?
- Share an example of how you can put others first this week.
- Why is this theory of "I am number one" wrong?
- What is people's biggest need?
- How are people's real needs and perceived needs sometimes different?
- How can you help to meet other people's real needs?
- How does verse five connect to Paul's instruction not to be selfish?

Cross-References

Mark 12:30-31 – Love the Lord your God with all your heart and with all your soul and with all your mind and with all your strength.' The second is this: 'Love your neighbor as yourself.' There is no commandment greater than these."

3 John 1:4 – I have no greater joy than to hear that my children are walking in the truth.

Romans 12:10 – Be devoted to one another in love. Honor one another above yourselves.

1 Peter 5:5 – In the same way, you who are younger, submit yourselves to your elders. All of you, clothe yourselves with humility toward one another, because, "God opposes the proud but shows favor to the humble."

Galatians 5:13 – You, my brothers and sisters, were called to be free. But do not use your freedom to indulge the flesh; rather, serve one another humbly in love.

Matthew 11:29 – Take my yoke upon you and learn from me, for I am gentle and humble in heart, and you will find rest for your souls.

Teaching Points

1. Verse 1-2 - "*If there is any encouragement in Christ, any comfort from love, any participation in the Spirit, any affection and sympathy, complete my joy by being of the same mind, having the same love, being in full accord and of one mind.*"

Paul is saying, "If any of these things are true, then respond in the right way by unifying together." You have all been encouraged in Christ. You have all been comforted by His love. You have all received the Holy Spirit. You are all recipients of this grace, so don't be divided; serve the Lord together.

So, to paraphrase Paul's words, "If Christ has done anything for you, if you have received His love, if you have benefited from the Spirit, if you have received any compassion from Christ, then make my joy full by being unified."

Certainly, all these things were true. Christ had done so much for them; they should respond by realizing that they were all equal recipients of God's grace and deciding to work together for the Lord.

2. We see again where Paul's heart is. His joy does not come from materials, achievements, awards, or compliments. His joy is to see believers growing to be more Christ-like.

Application: What kind of things make you happy? Real happiness does not come from wealth or materials. Joy is found in serving God and seeing others serve Him.

3. Paul's exhortation to unity - It seems almost every epistle by Paul stresses unity. Not everyone places a high value on unity. Many people focus more on doctrines and creeds. While these are important, unity cannot be ignored.

Jesus Himself prayed for unity for believers in John 17:20-22, "*I do not ask for these only, but also for those who will believe in me through their word, that they may all be one, just as you, Father, are in me, and I in you, that they also may be in us, so that the world may believe that you have sent me. The glory that you have given me I have given to them, that they may be one even as we are one.*"

And Paul said in Ephesians 4:3, "*being diligent to preserve the unity of the Spirit in the bond of peace.*"

Jesus knew that the future church would be fractured and divided, so he prayed for unity. Paul knew that unity is extremely difficult to maintain, so believers need to diligently keep it. Note that he says "preserve." Unity already belongs to believers based on our mutual relationship with Christ. We just need to maintain what is already there.

Unity is vital because the church can accomplish much more as a team working together than a bunch of individuals doing their own thing and disagreeing while at it.

Thinking of a soccer team, imagine that it is full of divisions and arguments. The forwards like one style of play and argue with the midfielders, who, in turn, are arguing with both the forwards and the defenders, who are blaming the goalie. Even in the middle of the game and before and after the game, they are voicing their loud disagreements. What will the result be?

They won't have any cohesion or teamwork. They won't be in the right places, and their team will lose games to even much less talented teams. They will have the most success if they all put aside their own preferences for how to play the game and follow who? The coach. The team needs one cohesive plan of action. They need unity.

Arguments among believers keep us from the more vital task of sharing the gospel and making disciples. Besides that, division hurts the church's testimony, so others don't want to listen as much to what we say.

Application: What are some specific examples of how you can work hard to maintain unity? Is there anything that you should divide with others over? What kinds of things should you *not* divide over?

4. Verses 3-4 - *Do nothing from selfish ambition or conceit, but in humility count others more significant than yourselves. Let each of you look not only to his own interests, but also to the interests of others.*

These are two of the most well-known verses in the New Testament. Imagine what the world would be like if everybody followed this verse, doing "nothing from selfish ambition," but looking after the interests of others.

Selfishness is the root of almost all sin. Greed, envy, murder, adultery, lying, stealing, and gluttony are just a few of the sins that stem from selfishness. We could go on and on. If only believers would follow this principle, the world would be a much better place!

The problem is that we all love ourselves. We all have the selfish tendency to put our wants and desires above others. While it is difficult to eradicate all selfishness from our lives immediately, how can we start to achieve this goal?

Firstly, we can make it a habit to examine our actions. Stop to think about why we are doing what we are doing. Sometimes we react and just do things without really thinking them through. So, if we would evaluate our own thoughts, we could recognize selfish ones and then actively decide not to pursue those original selfish ideas.

Secondly, we can think of specific areas where we tend to be selfish.

Application: What is one area you tend to struggle with selfishness? What can you do this week to put others first in this area?

Thirdly, we can come to the Word to see ourselves as we really are and pray to the Lord for strength to be more like Him.

Fourthly, we can actively look for ways to serve others. Serving others does not usually happen naturally. We need to keep our eyes open and be observant to watch for opportunities to serve. This is precisely the opposite of human tendency, which is to try to remain ignorant about what we can do to help others out.

While riding public transport, on many occasions, I have seen young men notice the elderly out of the corner of their eyes and then close their eyes and pretend to sleep, so they don't have to give up their seats.

Application: How about in your home? Do you ever notice a full trash can or a sink full of dishes and then walk along, hoping that your spouse will see and take care of it first? Write out five specific ways you can look out for others' interests in the coming week.

5. The phrase "do not merely" tells us that, in fact, everyone will look out for their own interests. This is natural. Some will teach we should make sure to love ourselves, but this is not a problem for anyone. Everybody does this

already. The issue is that we love ourselves to the exclusion of others or more than others. We are commanded in Mark 12:31 to love others as we love ourselves. This also implies that everyone does love himself.

Looking out for number one will not give you joy. The word JOY can be taken as an acronym.

J - Jesus
O - Others
Y - Yourself

To have true joy, you should put Jesus first, others second, and yourself last.

Jesus is our ultimate example. Of all people who ever lived, He gave up the most in service of others. Christ actually was more important than others (whereas we are equal to others in God's sight). He had a much higher rank than anyone He served. He genuinely had inherent rights and privileges, whereas we only think we have rights. Yet of all people, He was the one who was truly humble. Considering others more important than Himself, He gave up His own divine rights in order to serve others.

II. Christological doctrinal passage on the incarnation of Christ (6-8)

Discussion Questions

- What does it mean "he existed in the form of God"?
- Was Jesus equal with God?
- Was He still equal with God when He came to earth and became a man?
- What does it mean that he didn't regard equality with God a thing to be grasped?
- Explain the phrase "emptied himself." Did Christ empty Himself of

deity? Did He exchange deity for humanity?

- Did Jesus truly become a man? Why is the doctrine of the incarnation important?
- What does the phrase "found in appearance as a man" imply? (There was something more, not less, to His humanity. That is, He was also deity at the same time.)
- What was unique about death on a cross that made it singled out here?
- Share one area you can imitate Christ's example of service and humility in the coming week.

Cross References

Colossians 1:15-17 – The Son is the image of the invisible God, the firstborn over all creation. For in him all things were created: things in heaven and on earth, visible and invisible, whether thrones or powers or rulers or authorities; all things have been created through him and for him. He is before all things, and in him all things hold together.

Hebrews 1:2-3 – But in these last days he has spoken to us by his Son, whom he appointed heir of all things, and through whom also he made the universe. The Son is the radiance of God's glory and the exact representation of his being, sustaining all things by his powerful word. After he had provided purification for sins, he sat down at the right hand of the Majesty in heaven.

John 5:18 - For this reason they tried all the more to kill him; not only was he breaking the Sabbath, but he was even calling God his own Father, making himself equal with God.

John 10:33 - "We are not stoning you for any good work," they replied, "but for blasphemy, because you, a mere man, claim to be God."

Matthew 20:28 – Just as the Son of Man did not come to be served, but to serve, and to give his life as a ransom for many.

1 Timothy 2:5 – For there is one God and one mediator between God and

mankind, the man Christ Jesus.

Hebrews 4:15 – For we do not have a high priest who is unable to empathize with our weaknesses, but we have one who has been tempted in every way, just as we are—yet he did not sin.

Teaching Points

1. Who is Jesus? - This passage is one of the most important doctrines in the Bible. It tells us the nature of Jesus, both His divine and His human nature. It communicates the details about the incarnation, addressing fundamental theological questions. "Who is Jesus?" is a crucial question, as the whole crux of the gospel is to believe in Him. Who do we believe in? This passage gives us not only the answer to this question, but also some very practical points as to how we must model the humility He showed in our own lives.

2. Verse 6 - Philippians 2:6, "*who, though he was in the form of God, did not count equality with God a thing to be grasped.*"

In the NASB version, it says that He "existed" in the form of God. The word, "existed," denotes Jesus' continuous state both then and now. He is eternally existent, and there was never a time when He didn't exist.

The "form of God" doesn't just mean that Jesus looks like God or is the same shape, but rather it teaches that Jesus's very essence is the same as God's. In other words, Jesus is eternally God. There was never a point in time when He wasn't God and became God; neither is there a point in time when He was God and then ceased to be God. How is this possible? God is a Trinity with three distinct but unified and equal beings. Although Jesus is eternally God, He didn't hold on to His rights as God.

<u>One of the most important teachings of the gospel is that Jesus is 100% God and 100% man.</u>

3. Jesus emptied Himself -

These words are very important to the doctrine of the incarnation. First of all, there was no outside power at work that overcame Jesus and weakened Him. Jesus made a voluntary decision to set aside certain aspects of His deity for a time and purpose. It doesn't mean He didn't have these divine abilities or that He could not use them. Otherwise, the logical conclusion of that would be that He ceased to be God for a span of time.

Rather, He chose not to make use of certain aspects of His deity. For example?

- His glory - The disciples caught a glimpse of this glory during the transfiguration when He revealed His true state to them.
- His own authority - On earth, He submitted Himself fully to the Father's will.
- Extreme riches - In heaven, He owned everything, but on earth, He was poor.
- Omnipresence - He was still aware of everything happening everywhere and could heal over distance but, at the same time, limited Himself to existing in one physical location.
- His intimate relationship with the Father - He gave up this fellowship with the Father on the cross when He took on the sins of the world and said, "My God, My God, why have you forsaken me?"

While Jesus was on earth and living as one of us, He set aside certain divine rights.

It is something akin to the tale of the Prince and the Pauper, a famous story in which a prince leaves the castle to become a commoner for bit. During that time, he doesn't have access to his money, his authority, or his army. The prince becomes poor and needs to work for food. He doesn't cease to be a prince, but he does set aside those privileges for a while.

4. Jesus became a bond-servant - He did not come the first time to rule or demand people to serve Him. He did not come to be served, but to serve (Mark 10:45). Jesus gave us the ultimate example of service when He stooped down to wash the disciple's feet. If Jesus can lower Himself to serve

others, how much more should we.

Application: What is one way you enjoy other people serving you? What is one way you can serve others in the coming week?

5. Jesus was made in the likeness of men - Jesus literally became a man. This is the essence of the incarnation. He became the God man, 100% man, 100% God. This is one of those doctrines in the Bible that is difficult to grasp because of our limitations. It will never be possible for us to completely comprehend God, who is so far beyond our own understanding. It is hard for us to fathom how Jesus could be fully God and man simultaneously. Yet it is true. God is eternal spirit. Man is a body plus a spirit. Jesus came as a body plus an eternal spirit. So, He satisfies the definition of both God and man.

We see that Jesus had both a human nature (he grew tired, ate, slept, walked, talked, etc.) and a divine nature (healed over distance, healed outside of time, turned water into wine, had power over nature, power over sickness, power over death, etc.)

One of the first places to look at if you are unsure if a certain fellowship has right teaching or is a cult is their view of Jesus. It is one of the key places cults tend to go off. Some of the common heresies about Christ include:

1. He is only a god (Arianism, Jehovah's Witnesses).
2. He was created by God and is the highest of all God's creation.
3. He was only a man that was somehow indwelt by the Spirit of God. Kind of like a shell taken over by something else.
4. He was not actually a man; his body was a kind of apparition.
5. He somehow became God later in His life when he reached a certain spiritual level, perhaps at His baptism.

All of these are heresies are taught by people who deny the Word of God, and we should watch out for them or any other variation that denies either Jesus's deity or His humanity.

34

6. The purpose of the incarnation was for Jesus to die on the cross (verse 8) -

Dying to take away our sins was the whole purpose for Jesus to become a man. It wasn't because He wanted to see what it was like or experience something new. Jesus died to save us from our sins. Becoming a man was a necessary part of God's plan by which Christ could act as our representatives, as Adam did in the garden. His death was not just an ordinary death but the most shameful and torturous kind. This is where His obedience and humility led Him. Jesus looked into the future and knew exactly where His decision to become a man would take Him, still choosing to follow that path, even knowing the pain it would bring.

Application: Are you willing to obey God even if it leads to personal sacrifice?

III. Christological doctrinal passage on the exaltation of Christ (9-11)

Discussion Questions

- Is there any relationship between Jesus' humiliation and His exultation?
- What general Biblical principle does this teach?
- What is the name that Paul refers to here?
- Will atheists bow the knee to Christ? When?
- How about Buddhists, Muslims, agnostics, demons, Satan?
- What does bowing the knee signify?
- What will happen to unbelievers after they bow the knee and confess if that doesn't take place until after their death?
- What happens if we confess now instead of later?
- What, then, should our response be to these truths?

Cross-References

Revelation 20:11-13 - Then I saw a great white throne and him who was seated on it. The earth and the heavens fled from his presence, and there was no place for them. And I saw the dead, great and small, standing before the throne, and books were opened. Another book was opened, which is the book of life. The dead were judged according to what they had done as recorded in the books.

Romans 10:9-10 – If you declare with your mouth, "Jesus is Lord," and believe in your heart that God raised him from the dead, you will be saved. For it is with your heart that you believe and are justified, and it is with your mouth that you profess your faith and are saved.

Philippians 2:12 - Therefore, my dear friends, as you have always obeyed—not only in my presence, but now much more in my absence—continue to work out your salvation with fear and trembling

James 4:10 - Humble yourselves before the Lord, and he will lift you up.

Teaching Points

1. Jesus' exaltation - Christ's humiliation and subsequent exaltation are connected together and predestined before the world even began. It is the ultimate example of the principle taught in James 4:10 that if you "*humble yourselves before the Lord...he will lift you up.*"

No one went from any higher to lower than Jesus. And no one will ever go from lower to higher. He started off in the highest position in the universe. And He lowered Himself to the lowest rank (becoming all sin of all time for us), after which He was once again raised to the highest position. The Father did this to exalt His son and to show us, through action, how important humility is.

It is not immediately clear what the "name which is above every name" refers to. Some scholars believe it refers to the name "Lord," which signifies Jesus' position over all things and people. This interpretation fits with verse 11, which says that one day "every tongue [will] confess that Jesus Christ is **Lord**."

2. One day every person will be a believer - All people will finally admit that Jesus is Lord. Many defy Him now and say the most horrid things about God. Yet one day, they, too, will bow their knee to Jesus. Hitler will bow. Stalin will bow. Richard Dawkins will bow his knee to Jesus and say, "You are Lord." Your relatives who laugh at your beliefs and your co-workers who scoff at you will all bow the knee to Jesus. All Buddhists, Muslims, Jews, Hindus, evolutionists, and atheists will proclaim that Jesus is Lord.

Application: Every person must do this. There is no escaping it. You can either do this voluntarily in your life now and receive eternal life or by force right before the final judgment. Bowing the knee to Jesus is also not a one-time thing. Yes, salvation happens at a specific point when we first bow our knees to Jesus and confess that He is our Lord. But after that, living a life to please God requires bowing to His will daily. We must live each day and make each decision acknowledging His authority over our lives. How can you bow the knee to Jesus this week?

Philippians 2:12-30

Outline

I. Christian Living Applications (12-18)
II. Paul's plans to send Timothy and Epaphroditus (19-30)

I. Christian Living Applications (12-18)

Discussion Questions

- What does it show about the Philippians that they obeyed whether Paul was there or not?
- What does it mean to work out your salvation?
- Why with fear and trembling?
- What is the relationship of this instruction to the previous passage?
- How does verse 13 relate to verse 12?
- How can it help believers knowing that God is also at work in us?
- Why does God do this work?
- Share an example of a situation that tempts you to grumble or complain.
- Explain the phrase "prove yourselves" from verse 15. Prove to whom?
- How can you shine as a light in the world? Share an example of a way to shine the light.
- What is the word of life? How can you "hold fast" to it?
- What does Paul's running/toiling refer to? Why were these not in vain? What kind of life is in vain?
- What is the world toiling after? What about you?

Cross-References

John 14:15 - If you love me, you will keep my commandments.

James 1:22 - But be doers of the word, and not hearers only, deceiving yourselves.

2 Corinthians 13:5 - Examine yourselves, to see whether you are in the faith. Test yourselves. Or do you not realize this about yourselves, that Jesus Christ is in you?—unless indeed you fail to meet the test!

Lamentations 3:40 - Let us test and examine our ways, and return to the Lord!

James 5:9 - Do not grumble against one another, brothers, so that you may not be judged; behold, the Judge is standing at the door.

Matthew 5:14-16 - You are the light of the world. A city set on a hill cannot be hidden. Nor do people light a lamp and put it under a basket, but on a stand, and it gives light to all in the house. In the same way, let your light shine before others, so that they may see your good works and give glory to your Father who is in heaven.

Teaching Points

1. The Philippians obeyed - In verse 12, Paul gives quite the compliment to the Philippians. He says that they "have always obeyed." And they have obeyed whether or not Paul was physically present with them. That is the mark of true obedience. Many children may act obedient when their parent or teacher is present, but then when they are alone, their behavior may be markedly different. A person who is truly obedient to God obeys regardless of who is or isn't watching.

Application: Is your behavior different when others are around compared to when you are alone? If the answer is "yes," then you also need to evaluate why that is the case. If you act one way in front of one group and another way in front of a different group or by yourself, then most likely, your motivation is wrong. It could be that you are motivated by a desire to please others or look good instead of wanting to please God.

2. Work out your salvation with fear and trembling - The command here to "work out your salvation" goes back to verses 10-11. In those verses, we saw that every person will one day bow the knee to Jesus and confess He is Lord. This will either happen voluntarily now or, if people refuse to bow themselves, then one day God will force them to. If a person is not saved, judgment in hell will follow their forced acknowledgment of Christ. And that is why Paul says to "work out your salvation." In other words, "make sure you are saved!"

Application: Every believer should periodically perform self-examination. Do not rely on a decision that you made when you were a child or when you raised your hand during an altar call. I do not mean that those decisions are invalid. Once a person is saved, he is always saved (John 10:27-30). However, many people are not saved but think they are (Matthew 7:21). Some people are living sinful and selfish lifestyles while saying, "I am safe. I prayed the salvation prayer."

Jesus said that "every good tree bears good fruit" (Matthew 7:17-18.) If you are saved, there should be fruit in your life. Do you have a love for God? Do you have a lifestyle of obedience? Do you have a passion for the lost? Is your life typified by hatred of sin and a desire for holiness? Are you repentant when you sin? These are just some of the questions you should ask yourself when you examine your spiritual condition.

The most vital question you can ever ask yourself is, "Am I saved?"

There is a test that we can give ourselves in 1 John 3:9, "No one born of God practices sinning." So, the test is, "Am I practicing sin?"

We should use this test to examine our own lives to see where we fall short. Examine to see if our heart truly belongs to God. If we find that we are practicing sin, we must fall on our knees before God, repent, and STOP practicing sin. We could title this verse, "give yourself a spiritual self-exam."

So, I would ask, have you given yourself the self-exam? Have you really looked hard at these Scriptures and evaluated your actions by them?

Often, when people go for checkups, the doctor will tell them they are unhealthy. They are overweight. They are not eating well. They are not exercising well. The patient says, "yeah, yeah, yeah." Then on the way home, he buys a couple of Monster burgers, an order of French fries, and a large soda. He arrives home, plumps himself down on the couch, and flips on the TV. He continues on in the exact same lifestyle until what happens? He has a heart attack. I hope none of you will be like this patient. Perform this self-exam and then change your lifestyle accordingly. If none of us make any applications from this, we have wasted our time studying this chapter.

3. For it is God who works in you - Although we are supposed to examine ourselves and make sure we are saved, Paul does not say to "work hard for salvation." Salvation is always given as a gift of God through faith by grace. Salvation is God's work on our behalf. Jesus accomplished it through His death and resurrection. If you try to work to earn God's merit, whatever you do will never be enough.

In these two verses, we see once again the dual truths of man's responsibility and God's sovereignty taught side by side. God gives salvation, but we should ensure that we have truly received it through genuine faith.

4. Do all things without grumbling or disputing - Sometimes verses contain profound theological truth that is difficult to understand and requires much thought and study. Other times it is a simple application. This verse falls into the latter category. Every person can read this verse and know what it means (hint: it means that we should not grumble or argue). But doing it is another thing.

I can think over my life and remember certain things that have "set me off" and caused me to complain. Here are a few examples:

- Not being able to find something I need where I thought I put it (for example, a tool or document).
- Things breaking, like computers, phones, or door-knobs. I like things to

go smoothly and don't enjoy fixing things.
- People who are annoying, divisive, or demanding.
- Just missing the bus or the train.
- Inept and sinful governments.

I could go on. What is something that happens that tempts you to complain?

God's word is clear here. God does not want us to complain. Ever! About anything! It says to do **"all things"** without grumbling. Our sinful natures mean we have a bias toward complaining. It is much more natural for us to complain than it is for us to be thankful. Words of complaint flow far easier out of our mouths than words of appreciation.

Application: How can we better control what we say to make sure we don't complain? What is something that you sometimes complain about that you can thank God for now? How can we train ourselves so that gratitude will flow more easily than words of complaint?

5. Among whom you shine as lights in the world - The Philippians lived in the midst of a crooked and perverse generation, and so do we. Our mission from the Lord is to "shine as lights." Jesus told the disciples that He is the "light of the world" (John 8:12.) And another time, He said, "you are the light of the world" (Matthew 5:14.)

God calls us to be Christians, followers of Christ. We are to live differently than the worldly people around us. Instead of pursuing materials, money, fame, achievement, and pleasure, we pursue Christ. He is our authority. He is our standard. He is our pearl of great price.

The world is falling head over heels into relativism, which evil teachings like evolution only contribute to. Similar to the time of the judges, people do what is right in their own eyes. Traditional standards of right and wrong are being eroded before our eyes as people celebrate sin in many forms. Sin is not only tolerated, but it is promoted. And those who condemn it are labeled as bigots and are persecuted.

Against this backdrop, those who follow Christ live in stark contrast to the world. When we uncompromisingly follow His standard, we shine His light on a lost world. No, we don't walk around with actual halos. But our actions show people a better way, the Creator's way. The Word of God is a lamp to our feet and a light to our path, leading people in the right way. Similarly, your actions can lead people to God.

Application: If a neutral observer had unrestricted access to watch you live your life 24/7, would they conclude that you are much different from an unbeliever? Would they know you are a follower of Christ only through observing your actions?

6. Holding fast to the word of life - As we just read, we live in the midst of a crooked and perverse generation. All around us, people are preaching relative truth. They argue that what is right and true for one person is not for another. Standards constantly shift with the times. Views of basic concepts like gender and marriage have drastically altered in the last ten years. What is going to anchor you? How do you know anymore what is wrong and what is right? Many people simply follow the media's new flavor of the day. But Paul gives the solution. We must hold fast to the word of life.

God's Word is our anchor. He is our absolute moral standard. Not only does He give us direction, but He also strengthens us to "run" the race for Him. There may be times of doubt. From the very beginning, Satan tried to cast doubt into Adam and Eve's hearts saying, "Did God really say?" If they had held fast to the word of life, they could have resisted the temptation. But Eve allowed the seed of doubt to grow in her heart.

We must regularly come before the Lord through His Word and renew our minds. Do not let the seed of doubt grow within you. Hold fast to the anchor. Then you can stand immovable no matter how much the sands of culture in this world shift, swallowing up the foolish in the ever-changing quicksand of moral relativity.

7. I did not run in vain or labor in vain - After conversion, Paul invested his life in preaching the gospel, making disciples, and planting churches. He used

his time and gifts to build God's kingdom, focusing on things of eternal value. It is only natural that Paul did not want to see his efforts wasted. Hoping to have fruit that remained, he encouraged the Philippians to hold fast. Although Paul was not directly responsible for others' behavior, if the people he ministered to fell away, then he would have felt that he was laboring in vain. For his efforts to be proven worthwhile, the Philippians had to carry on in their faith.

Application: It should be the goal of each of us to bear fruit that will last the test of time. Whatever God has called you to do, you should establish it in such a way that it will continue even after you are gone. If you are called to an orphanage ministry, what will happen to that ministry if something happens to you? Will it continue? If you are leading a Bible study, will it endure if you can't teach anymore? Will your children still follow God once they grow up and you can't make them go to church anymore?

8. Even if I am poured out as a drink offering - This statement is a euphemism for martyrdom. Paul was in prison when he wrote this epistle, expecting that he might be executed for his faith at any time. While he was very willing to give his life for Christ, he did not want to see it given away for nothing! In some respect, the Philippian church was his legacy.

9. Mutual rejoicing - In Romans 12:15, Paul said to "rejoice with those who rejoice and weep with those who weep." Typically, when someone talks about rejoicing, they share good news. The birth of a new child, a wedding between believers, an answer to prayer--all of these are reasons to rejoice. But here, Paul mentions his potential martyrdom. He was able to rejoice, even facing possible death, knowing that he faithfully lived out God's calling for him and that there was fruit that would last. In turn, he asked the Philippians to also rejoice with him.

Paul's attitude here reminds us of when he was singing praise songs to God in prison with Silas (Acts 16:25.) Rejoicing through trials is a sign of close fellowship with and reliance upon God.

Application: Are you able to rejoice in the midst of trials? What is a trial you are facing now that you can rejoice in?

II. Paul's plans to send Timothy and Epaphroditus (19-30)

Discussion Questions

- Why did Paul think so highly of Timothy?
- What does the phrase "kindred spirit" mean?
- What was the problem with the other people Paul might have sent?
- What does the word "worker" convey about the life of a believer? How about soldier?
- Why is Epaphroditus called "your messenger"?
- Did the Philippians know him? How do you know?
- How did Epaphroditus's healing affect Paul?
- Why should they hold him in high regard?
- What does this verse tell us about how we should treat Christian workers in general?
- What is one Christian worker you know whom you could encourage and support?

Cross-References

1 Corinthians 10:24 - Let no one seek his own good, but the good of his neighbor.

Romans 12:10 - Love one another with brotherly affection. Outdo one another in showing honor.

Teaching Points

1. Timothy - Timothy was a faithful disciple and close partner of Paul. Paul

and Timothy teamed up to travel throughout the Middle East to make disciples and establish churches. Often, when Paul could not visit a church himself, he would send Timothy as a proxy. Timothy had proved himself to be trustworthy. Here, Paul gives him a big compliment: "I have no one like him who will be genuinely concerned for your welfare." Many people, even ministers of the gospel, have served with layers of their own motivations. Perhaps they sought popularity, financial return, or had other ulterior motives. Timothy was not like that. He selflessly cared for those whom he ministered to, proving that he was in it for them and not for himself.

Application: From Timothy, we learn the importance of servant leadership. A leader should lovingly and humbly serve the flock. A minister of the gospel should not serve for money or recognition or any other motives but purely to help God's people.

2. Epaphroditus - Epaphroditus was evidently a member of the Philippian church who had come from them as a messenger to Paul in order to minister to him in prison. He also very possibly brought a monetary gift for Paul to support his ministry. Not much is known about him except what is written here. He was a "fellow worker" and a "fellow soldier." Paul says that he "risked his life" to come and minister to him. Traveling long distances at that time was dangerous enough. But going to offer help to a "criminal" whom so many hated made his trip of love even more hazardous.

While visiting Paul, Epaphroditus came down with a sickness. His illness was severe, and he almost died. The Philippians were naturally very worried about their dear brother when they heard the news, so Paul decided to send him back to them.

Epaphroditus' story reminds us that there are many kinds of workers serving in God's kingdom. Not everyone is a Paul. Not all are called to be up front or famous. In the body of Christ, there are many types of people with many gifts and many callings. Paul's ministry would not have been nearly as effective without faithful people like Epaphroditus, who helped and encouraged him along the way. For every effective pastor, there is a group of other believers serving behind the scenes. Some teach Sunday School. Some business-people give offerings and share in their communities. Prayer warriors give their time to fight spiritual battles on their knees. Those with the gift of hospitality invite others to their home or make meals for the sick. There is a need for every type of gifting in building God's church.

Application: Are you actively serving the body of Christ and building God's kingdom? Share one way you can support or encourage others who are serving God (like Epaphroditus did) this week.

3. Honor such men - Churches should not "over-exalt" pastors. They should not be raised up on a pedestal above others. The hand is not exalted over the foot, right? Every believer's role is important. Men like Epaphroditus who serve in a more complimentary role should be respected as well.

Application: Share one thing from today's lesson you can apply in the coming week.

Philippians 3:1-11

Outline

I. Our fleshly achievements count as nothing (1-6)
II. All worldly things are nothing compared to knowing Christ (7-11)

I. Our fleshly achievements count as nothing (1-6)

Discussion Questions

- What same things is he referring to in verse 1?
- Why do biblical writers often repeat things many times?
- Who do the "dogs" refer to? Why does Paul call them dogs?
- What is the false circumcision?
- Why was this so dangerous?
- What, then, is the true circumcision?
- What is the key difference between the two groups?
- What do people of the true circumcision focus on?
- What does "flesh" refer to?
- Why can we put no confidence in the flesh?
- Is Paul boasting in verses 4-6?
- What is his point?
- If Paul could not rely on his earthly achievements, what does this say about us?
- What attitude should we have since we know we cannot merit God's favor?

Cross-References

Galatians 2:3 – Yet not even Titus, who was with me, was compelled to be

48

circumcised, even though he was a Greek.

Acts 15:1 – Certain people came down from Judea to Antioch and were teaching the believers: "Unless you are circumcised, according to the custom taught by Moses, you cannot be saved."

Romans 2:25-29 – Circumcision has value if you observe the law, but if you break the law, you have become as though you had not been circumcised. So then, if those who are not circumcised keep the law's requirements, will they not be regarded as though they were circumcised? The one who is not circumcised physically and yet obeys the law will condemn you who, even though you have the written code and circumcision, are a lawbreaker. A person is not a Jew who is one only outwardly, nor is circumcision merely outward and physical. No, a person is a Jew who is one inwardly; and circumcision is circumcision of the heart, by the Spirit, not by the written code. Such a person's praise is not from other people, but from God.

Romans 7:5 – For when we were in the realm of the flesh, the sinful passions aroused by the law were at work in us, so that we bore fruit for death.

Ephesians 2:1 - As for you, you were dead in your transgressions and sins

Genesis 17:12 – For the generations to come every male among you who is eight days old must be circumcised, including those born in your household or bought with money from a foreigner—those who are not your offspring.

Teaching Points

1. Rejoice in the Lord (1) - Paul again reminds the Philippians that they need to rejoice. He himself admits that he has told them this and these other issues before. Yet he also realizes it is necessary to remind them, as a way of protecting them. The same issues are repeated again and again in the Bible because God knows we are forgetful. The word "remember" occurs in the Bible 227 times. Much of the content in the Bible is review.

2. Review is important (1) - Paul repeats a lot of instructions to the churches

because reminders and review are necessary. It is like language learning. If you spend every day memorizing new lists but don't review the previous vocabulary lists, what will the result be? You will end up truly learning nothing. But if you spend 60-80% of the time on reviewing, you will end up retaining a lot more. Sometimes learners might feel in a rush to know new things, which is why Paul reminded them how necessary it was to repeat the same old things.

3. Look out for the dogs (2-3) - These verses refer to the problem of the Judaizers in the early church. The Judaizers were groups of legalistic Jews who claimed to believe in the gospel but added their own works and traditions to it. Their main doctrine was that you not only need to believe in Christ but must also keep the law, especially circumcision, or you cannot be saved.

Paul refers to this group as dogs (at the time, wild dogs roamed the streets of the cities in that area, causing havoc), evil workers (because they were doing the work of Satan), and the false circumcision (because they focused on external physical circumcision but ignored the heart, which was truly important). Paul often warned the church to watch out for these works-oriented groups.

There are many problems with a works-oriented approach. Here are a few:

- The biggest problem is that it cannot possibly be successful! They were teaching people to follow the law, but it is impossible for anyone to keep the whole law. That is one of the major points in the Old Testament and of preparing people for the coming of Christ. A person who tries to follow all of the laws in the Old Testament will fall far short. He will be burdened to the point of collapse. And finally, he will collapse under the strain that no man (except for Christ) can bear.

- It encourages pride. Most Jews were extremely prideful. They looked down on all the uncircumcised and trusted in themselves, thinking it was their works that would save them.

- It gives man the glory instead of God. It is no coincidence that in the next verse, Paul says true believers glory in Christ Jesus. Those who trust in their own works don't. In fact, they wouldn't even need Christ. So, while adding works seems like a small and even helpful addition to the gospel equation, it immediately makes things man-centric and negates the need for Christ.

4. True circumcision is circumcision of the heart - Circumcision of the heart refers to a heart that is set apart for and devoted to God, giving rise to a sincere faith in Christ. The rest of verse 3 also sheds further light on real circumcision. It is worshiping God (whereas works oriented approach focuses on man) and giving all the glory to Christ. That means, recognizing salvation comes from Christ alone. It is 100% Him and 0% us, not a fifty-fifty split.

It is also an understanding that the flesh avails nothing. There is no room for confidence in our own achievements or abilities. We put our confidence in Christ, not in ourselves. Many Jews felt that they were granted automatic entry into God's family simply because they were "good," circumcised Jews. Paul refutes that idea in these verses. The ones who actually belong to God are not those who are physically circumcised but those who worship Him, trust in Jesus, and put no confidence in their own flesh.

This last phrase, "no confidence in the flesh," is one of the major themes of the passage today. Nothing we do can take away our sins. None of our own achievements can bring us to God. It doesn't matter how many people we share with, how many Scriptures we memorize, how many times we have read the Bible, how many good deeds we have done, how many promotions we have gotten, how many exams we have aced, how many languages we have learned, how many houses/cars we have bought, how many friends we have made, how many patients' lives we have saved, how much of the Bible we have memorized, how many prayers we have said, or how many times we have visited church. We must put no confidence in these things or anything else of ourselves to bring us to God.

5. Paul gives himself as an example here (4-6) - Keep in mind that he is the

example of the ultimate Jew. The Judaizers taught that you need to follow the law and get circumcised in addition to trusting in Christ. Paul uses himself as an example that all of these things they were putting confidence in are not enough. He doesn't mention these things to boast. How do we know? Because he makes it clear that these worldly achievements are meaningless. He wasn't praising them. He was saying they are useless.

Paul's point is that by the Judaizer's own standards, he was the ultimate Jew. If anyone could save themselves by being a good Jew, it was Paul. However, all of these things, which good Jews thought necessary to do, actually led him away from God instead of to God. People were crushed under the weight of self-reliance and rules-based religion, none of which worked.

Matthew 1:29 - *Take my yoke upon you, and learn from me, for I am gentle and lowly in heart, and you will find rest for your souls.*

The yoke of the religion of good works is heavy and oppressive, but Jesus' yoke is light. He can give rest to weary souls.

Application: Make a list of your own most memorable achievements. Then pray before the Lord and humbly acknowledge that all of these things cannot bring you any closer to Him. Ask Him to make you humble and rely on Him rather than yourself.

II. All worldly things are nothing compared to knowing Christ (7-11)

Discussion Questions

- What does it mean that Paul has counted the things listed in verses 4-6 as loss?
- What are some earthly or religious achievements that you may need to

count as "loss"?

- What have you given up for the sake of following Christ? Was it worth it?
- Based on verses 7-8, does your perspective toward this world need to change? If so, how?
- What is Paul's goal in verse 9?
- What is the difference between righteousness that comes from following the law and the righteousness from God?
- What does it mean to "know" Him?
- What is the difference between this knowledge and how you might know an acquaintance?
- What specific ways are given that we should strive to know God more deeply in?
- What does "fellowship of His sufferings" mean?

Cross-References

Matthew 16:24-26 – Then Jesus said to his disciples, "Whoever wants to be my disciple must deny themselves and take up their cross and follow me. For whoever wants to save their life will lose it, but whoever loses their life for me will find it. What good will it be for someone to gain the whole world, yet forfeit their soul? Or what can anyone give in exchange for their soul?

Luke 14:33 – In the same way, those of you who do not give up everything you have cannot be my disciples.

Romans 12:1-2 – Therefore, I urge you, brothers and sisters, in view of God's mercy, to offer your bodies as a living sacrifice, holy and pleasing to God—this is your true and proper worship. Do not conform to the pattern of this world, but be transformed by the renewing of your mind. Then you will be able to test and approve what God's will is—his good, pleasing and perfect will.

John 17:3 – Now this is eternal life: that they know you, the only true God, and Jesus Christ, whom you have sent.

2 Corinthians 4:6 – For God, who said, "Let light shine out of darkness," made his light shine in our hearts to give us the light of the knowledge of God's glory displayed in the face of Christ.

Hebrews 4:15 – For we do not have a high priest who is unable to empathize with our weaknesses, but we have one who has been tempted in every way, just as we are—yet he did not sin.

Teaching Points

1. Whatever gain I had, I counted as loss for the sake of Christ (7) - Paul's conclusion about his past as the model Jew is here in verse 7. Before salvation, he considered these things valuable. Afterward, he considered them a loss. This is an accounting term for a business, meaning taking a hit. "Loss" means that these things weren't only neutral; they took him into the red territory, leading him farther away from what was truly important. Why?

These things led him farther from Christ because they caused him to become prideful in his own achievements. They caused him to rely on himself instead of placing his faith in Christ. This is why Paul said those who preach that such things are important are evil workers. These things of themselves aren't evil, but when we rely on them, they become evil because they take the place of God in our lives.

Satan often works in this way. He knows it would be hopeless to convince many Jews to go out and start murdering, stealing, and mugging people. He would be laughed out of town. Instead, he encouraged them to follow a lot of external traditions, try to gain society's respect, and do good deeds, knowing that they would soon believe that they were good and could deal with the sin problem by themselves. This temptation by Satan has been tremendously successful for centuries.

However, Paul, by the grace of God, came to a realization that these traditions increased the distance between him and God. He decided to mark them in the loss column, immediately forsake putting his confidence in them, and instead pursue things that were truly valuable.

Application: What is an example of a worldly thing you have pursued before (or are still pursuing) that you need to give up for the sake of following after Christ?

2. The surpassing worth of knowing Christ as my Lord (8) -

- What is the most valuable thing we can ever get?
- Could you truthfully say what Paul said in verse 8?
- What are some things that you are tempted to place more value on than your relationship with Christ?
- In comparison to your love for Christ, do you consider these things rubbish?

If you think Paul was too excessive in completely dismissing these seemingly good things, then you would be even more shocked at verse 8. What does he compare these things to in this verse? He compares them to rubbish. This word can even be translated as manure.

Isaiah 64:6 - *We have all become like one who is unclean, and all our righteous deeds are like a polluted garment. We all fade like a leaf, and our iniquities, like the wind, take us away.*

The very best that the world has to offer and the very best that we can achieve is rubbish compared to what is truly important, knowing Christ. We just need to see these worldly things as they truly are. We need to look at these things with the eyes of Christ.

Compared with knowing Christ, EVERYTHING is a loss. The meaning is clear. Christ is the most valuable thing we can have in our lives. You often sing this at church, and it is echoed in popular songs like "More Precious Than Silver" and "You Are My Hiding Place." Every time we sing such songs, we claim that Christ is the most important things in our lives. But do we live it out? Do our actions back it up?

Application: Actions speak louder than words. Do we exalt our own achievements or hold on to worldly things? Do we become prideful at what we have done for God? Do we really consider our worldly achievements to be trash?

We should be willing to put all of our money on the table and burn it if it keeps us from following Christ. Compared to knowing Christ, money is garbage. We are commanded to be good stewards, but we should never let money interfere with our relationship with Christ. We should never put anything else in that cherished position in our hearts.

What is one thing you can give up for Christ this week?

3. Not having a righteousness of my own that comes from the law -

If we truly value Christ and place our faith in Him instead of in ourselves, He will impute true righteousness to our account.

Romans 4:6 - *God imputes righteousness apart from works.*

Romans 4:3 - *Abraham believed God and it was credited to him as righteousness.*

Righteousness does not come about through our own hard work. God puts it on us after we place our faith in Him, making us righteous.

4. Knowing Him is deeper than hearing of His name or being familiar with His story (10) - Knowing God is a personal relationship and fellowship. It includes experiencing the power of the resurrection since if we are in Christ, we ourselves are alive from the dead. It involves identifying ourselves with Christ and therefore sharing in His sufferings, meaning that we have some taste of the persecutions that He went through.

Also, knowing God means we follow Jesus' example of giving His life by dying to ourselves and living for Christ. We can develop a deep, personal connection to Christ if we truly have faith in Him through prayer and the Word.

5. Paul hoped to attain to the resurrection of the dead (11) -

Daniel 12:2 - *And many of those who sleep in the dust of the earth shall awake, some to everlasting life, and some to shame and everlasting contempt.*

The final resurrection is taught throughout the Bible. As Daniel wrote, some people would arise again to punishment and some to eternal life. Paul hoped to be in the second category! All these earthly achievements and even his fellow Jews' opinion of him was nothing compared to the hope of the resurrection. Would he face eternal punishment or eternal life? That is the question. Nothing else is important. Compared with one's eternal destiny, everything else in life fades to complete insignificance.

Application: How can you make sure that you will be resurrected to eternal life? How can you make sure of your salvation?

Philippians 3:12-21

Outline

I. Pressing on toward the goal (12-16)
II. Watch out for the enemies of Christ who set their minds on earthly things (17-19)
III. Our citizenship is in heaven (20-21)

I. Pressing on toward the goal (12-16)

Discussion Questions

- Paul says I press on to make "it my own." What does "it" refer to?
- What is Paul pressing on to lay hold of?
- Can we become perfect in this world? If it's not possible, what was Paul shooting for?
- He mentions "pressing on" or "reaching forward" three times in these verses. What does this mean?
- What is involved in pressing on to become sanctified?
- What kind of actions might someone take who is pressing on for holiness?
- How can you press on for this in your own life?
- What changes can you make?
- Why is it important to forget what is behind?
- How could not forgetting the past hinder future service to God?
- What are the similarities between what Paul is talking about here and an athlete?
- What is the prize Paul can get if he achieves his goal?
- What prize/reward are you striving for?
- What does it take for an athlete to win at a world-class level, like in the

Olympics? What is one way you can make more effort to strive for the goal?

Cross-References

2 Thessalonians 2:13-15 – But we ought always to thank God for you, brothers and sisters loved by the Lord, because God chose you as firstfruits to be saved through the sanctifying work of the Spirit and through belief in the truth. He called you to this through our gospel, that you might share in the glory of our Lord Jesus Christ. So then, brothers and sisters, stand firm and hold fast to the teachings we passed on to you, whether by word of mouth or by letter.

Proverbs 24:16 – For though the righteous fall seven times, they rise again, but the wicked stumble when calamity strikes.

1 John 1:9 – If we confess our sins, he is faithful and just and will forgive us our sins and purify us from all unrighteousness.

1 John 1:7 – But if we walk in the light, as he is in the light, we have fellowship with one another, and the blood of Jesus, his Son, purifies us from all sin.

Hebrews 8:12 – For I will forgive their wickedness and will remember their sins no more.

Psalms 102:12 – But you, Lord, sit enthroned forever; your renown endures through all generations.

Hebrews 12:2 – And let us run with perseverance the race marked out for us, fixing our eyes on Jesus, the pioneer and perfecter of faith. For the joy set before him he endured the cross, scorning its shame, and sat down at the right hand of the throne of God.

1 Corinthians 9:24- - Do you not know that in a race all the runners run, but only one gets the prize? Run in such a way as to get the prize.

Teaching Points

1. Summary - Below is a summary of this passage.

A. Paul realizes he hasn't achieved sanctification yet. He, like all believers, is on the way.

B. God chose Paul for the purpose of sanctifying him. This is why God chose all of us.

C. Although we may never achieve perfection in this world, it should still be our goal. Aim high. Miss high.

D. This is an athletic illustration. Like athletes, we are to press on for the finish line.

E. We are not to be complacent believers. We are to push forward, onward, and upward.

2. Paul has not yet obtained perfection - Paul recognized that he hadn't yet reached the goal. He wasn't yet holy. He wasn't yet perfect. Although this seems obvious, it is important for each of us to come to the same realization.

It is effortless to become complacent, especially for those of us who have been saved for a long time. We get into a groove of living the Christian life by habit. Going to church, reading the Bible, and even praying may become second nature. When we do all of these things, we start to think we have arrived, that we are good Christians.

But a key to living a holy life is to understand that you haven't arrived yet. There is always room for growth in every single area of our lives. If we pridefully think that we are "pretty good" or get into the habit of comparing ourselves with others, then we will not grow. And from this passage, we see that every believer needs to continually push forward to grow more like Christ each day.

Application: We need to humble ourselves. The first step is to admit to God and ourselves that we haven't arrived. Instead of comparing ourselves to others and thinking about how spiritual we are, we need to have a passion for holiness. What is one area of your Christian life in which you have become complacent? How can you renew your energy in that area to grow this week?

3. Forget successes -

Philippians 3:13b - "But one thing I do ,forgetting what lies behind and straining forward to what lies ahead."

There are two aspects of this verse. The first is to forget, forget the past. Paul's point is not that we cannot learn from the past. He is not saying, "wake up with amnesia each day." He is saying that we should not live in the past.

It could be that you did very well yesterday in your Christian walk. Perhaps you woke up early, spent one hour in prayer and Bible reading, and were patient and kind all day toward your family, serving them with a humble heart. On top of that, maybe you resisted temptation, immediately forgave those who offended you, sang praise songs all day, shared the gospel with five people, and gave your spouse a surprise dinner of their favorite food. Then in the evening, you memorized ten verses, prayed for another hour, and finally went to sleep. Does that sound like your day yesterday?

Even if it does, today is a new day. You cannot wake up today and say, "Yesterday I did well so today I will relax." Maybe last year you completed a read the Bible in a year plan. It's not last year anymore. Maybe last month you completed your application each week in your Bible study group. It is not last month anymore. Maybe last week you had a good time of prayer with the Lord each day. It is not last week anymore. Today starts a new week. Forget what is behind. Do not rest on your laurels.

Application: Is there a success in your past that is hindering you from moving forward? Perhaps something that gives you great pride? Beware that Satan will use this to attack you, building up your ego or tempting you to be lazy because you did so well in the past. Take it to God, confess your pride, and ask Him to show you what new goal He would have you work toward.

4. Forget failures - But maybe when you think of your past, you don't think of successes. Maybe failures come to mind. Maybe yesterday was a bad day. Maybe you got up late and said, "I will read the Bible at night before I sleep," and so you skipped it in the morning. Maybe you had a short temper with your kids and with your spouse. Maybe you complained about the trials you are facing. Maybe you fell into temptation. You argued with your spouse. And when you went to bed, you were so tired you skipped Bible reading and prayer again and said, "tomorrow."

Whether you failed yesterday or there was some other failure in your past, you might have woken up today feeling guilty. You may be reliving this past failure. It may be chaining you and holding you back from the future God wants for you. You should learn from it and grow from it. But today is a new day. 2020 is not 2019. You have new opportunities to serve God. His grace is more than enough to cover and wash away all of your past sins and failures. Forget what is behind you and push forward.

Application: Is there a failure in your life that you are reliving? A mistake that is holding you back from what God has for you today? Take it to God. Confess that sin once and for all. Move forward. Press on.

5. Straining forward / pressing on toward the goal - The second aspect of verse 13 (which is continued in verse 14) is to strain forward to what lies ahead. There will be a time to rest. But it is not now.

Hebrews 4:9, 11 - *So then, there remains a Sabbath rest for the people of God, Let us therefore strive to enter that rest, so that no one may fall by the same sort of disobedience.*

So, we are not to rest now. We need to zealously push forward.

Push forward to what? We press on toward the goal for the prize of the upward call.

What is the prize?

What are we straining for?

I believe the answer is coming into Jesus' presence in heaven. The most glorious moment I look forward to is when Jesus welcomes me into His arms in heaven and says, "well done, good and faithful servant." Are you looking forward to that? In a word, our prize is "Jesus." We get to have a relationship with Him. He has done everything for us. Therefore, we press on living each new day by His grace and to the best of our ability to please Him, knowing that one day we will see Him face to face.

We are in a race. This is not a race against the clock or against actual competitors where only one person wins. Every believer can win this race by claiming the resources God has given to us. We can all win the prize.

How do you feel after finishing a job well (e.g., finally completing a tough exam, fixing something that was broken, achieving a goal, deep cleaning your house, etc.)? It feels good. It is satisfying to do a job and do it well. This is similar to the feeling we have when we please the Lord and follow Him faithfully.

There is no higher calling than to please God--obeying Him each day, telling others about Him, glorifying Him in words and actions, and fulfilling His calling for our lives.

Application: Straining forward or pressing on conveys the idea of exerting oneself and expending a lot of energy in order to achieve the goal. What area of your life do you need to expend more energy to pursue God? What is one way you can do this?

There is a lot of athletic imagery here. Athletes have to train hard in order to be able to win. It is difficult. It takes hard work and dedication. The lazy never become winners. When that finish line draws near, a good athlete is trained not to let up but to strain forward for that finish line, using every ounce of energy left for one final push to cross that line. And that is how Christians are to pursue sanctification.

Remember – God is a God of new things: a new life, new beginning, new covenant, new hearts, and a new way of doing things. Because He is a God of new things, there is always hope and future. There is joy and peace. However, for the new things to begin, the old has to go away.

6. Let those who are mature think this way (15) - Every mature believer should have the same mindset as Paul describes here. This earth is not the place for followers of Jesus to rest or become complacent. The Christian life is not a lazy life. God wants us to be like an athlete, working hard to push forward to the goal.

In other words, the first battle is in the mind. If you lose the battle there, then your actions will quickly follow behind. Athletes that continually say, "I am tired. I need to rest," will never win anything. Neither will a believer who is complacent.

II. Watch out for the enemies of Christ who set their mind on earthly things (17-19)

Discussion Questions

- Why would Paul set himself up as their example? Was this prideful?
- Isn't Christ our only example?
- Why is it beneficial to observe others who follow this pattern?
- Who is one person that has modeled one aspect of the Christian life to you? How did that impact you?
- What is one thing you can model to other younger believers?

- Who are the enemies of the cross of Christ?
- Are all enemies of the cross Satanists?
- Where do we encounter enemies of God?
- What does it mean that their god is their appetite?

Cross-References

1 Corinthians 11:1 – Follow my example, as I follow the example of Christ.

1 Timothy 6:12 – Fight the good fight of the faith. Take hold of the eternal life to which you were called when you made your good confession in the presence of many witnesses.

James 4:4 - You adulterous people, don't you know that friendship with the world means enmity against God? Therefore, anyone who chooses to be a friend of the world becomes an enemy of God.

1 John 2:15 – Do not love the world or anything in the world. If anyone loves the world, love for the Father is not in them.

Teaching Points

1. Join in imitating me - Paul sets himself up as an example to the Philippians. It was not done out of pride. It is clear in these verses that Paul longed for the Philippians' growth in Christ. He wasn't making himself an example to boast or to solicit praise. Instead, he was doing it to give the Philippians a tangible, flesh-and-blood model to follow. This would help them in their spiritual walk.

Learning by example is one of the most powerful models of learning and, often, far more effective than lecturing. I have taught my children many things, many of these by example. Here are a few:

- I taught them how to tie their shoes by having them watch and imitate my movements.
- I taught them how to swim by modeling the strokes over and over.

- I taught my boys how to do push-ups by showing them good form.
- I taught them how to make paper airplanes by showing them and having them practice.
- One day, I will teach them how to tie ties or drive cars, also by modeling.

Few people would say modeling these things for my children is prideful. In like manner, Paul was not being prideful when he modeled aspects of spiritual life to his spiritual children.

Before we go and do likewise, we should evaluate our hearts and make sure we are humble and truly focused on the well-being of others. Certainly, pride can creep in as it did with the Pharisees.

And yet mature believers should model many aspects of following Christ for young believers. Here are some examples:

- Model how to have a quiet time.
- Model how to share the gospel.
- Model how to lead an inductive Bible study.
- Model how to repent after sinning.
- Model how to show hospitality.

Jesus modeled many things for the disciples. He showed them how to thank God before eating. He demonstrated the importance of quiet time alone with God in prayer. He showed them how to rebuke the proud, show compassion to the sinner, and respond to hate with love. It was Jesus' model on the cross that led Stephen likewise to say, "forgive them for they know not what they do."

Scripture is the final authority. But it is immensely helpful for us to see people model how to live out Scripture in their daily lives. And it is beneficial to see imperfect sinners do this because we, too, are imperfect.

2. For many walk as enemies of the gospel of Christ - This is given as a reason why it is important for believers to follow the right model. Jesus warned us that many will come as wolves dressed in sheep's clothing. It is

not only their teachings that will mislead people but their lifestyle.

Paul is very concerned that such people will mislead the Philippians. Thus, he asks them to follow his example and not theirs.

One example we can see of this in the world today is prosperity gospel preachers. They give a model of smooth speech, flashy lights, tailored clothes, private airplanes, greed, and living a life of luxury on the back of donations. Some might be swayed by their examples, thinking there is much profit in following God.

And that is why true preachers and teachers of the Bible need to give a better example, an example of humility, service, and self-sacrifice.

3. Their end is destruction - It may look like they are profiting for a while. Everything is going smoothly. But it will not last.

In Psalm 73, Asaph is confused about the seeming prosperity of the wicked. He struggles with why their life is so smooth. And his crisis of doubt almost leads him to fall away from God. But he comes into the temple and takes his concerns to God. In Psalm 73:17, he realizes the answer.

Psalms 73:17 - *Until I went into the sanctuary of God; then I discerned their end.*

The answer Asaph received was simple. In verse 17, he says, "then I perceived their end." He goes on to say, "you set them in slippery places. You cast them down to destruction. They are destroyed in a moment... utterly swept away by sudden terrors! Like a dream when one awakens."

Eventually, sooner or later, the wicked will receive justice for the wrongs they have done. They will not take their riches with them after death. One day each person will face God as the judge and must give an account for everything he has done. The security that their riches seem to provide is short-lived and has no real security at all.

While their lives seem to be smooth and easy, destruction comes upon them in a moment. Asaph's description reminds us of Jesus' parable about the rich fool, who did not know that he was about to die and that all of the things he so carefully stored up would avail him nothing. Money is but for a moment. A life built on things of this world is on a slippery slope. Only a life built on the rock of Christ is safe and sound.

4. Their god is their belly - This likely refers to their sensual desires and fleshly appetites. These enemies of Christ worship their own desires and pleasures. Just as a hungry person is motivated to fill his stomach, so they are motivated to satisfy their carnal longings.

In contrast, believers are to hunger for righteousness.

Matthew 5:6 - *Blessed are those who hunger and thirst for righteousness, for they shall be filled.*

III. Our citizenship is in heaven (20-21)

Discussion Questions

- What is an example of an earthly thing that you sometimes set your mind on?
- What does it mean to you that our citizenship is in heaven?
- Knowing this, how should we act while we are on earth?
- If you were to leave your country and move abroad, what might you miss?
- Do you think about heaven?
- Do you long for anything there?
- What is one way you can be heavenly minded this week?

Cross-References

Colossians 3:2 – Set your minds on things above, not on earthly things.

Romans 12:1-2 – Therefore, I urge you, brothers and sisters, in view of God's mercy, to offer your bodies as a living sacrifice, holy and pleasing to God—this is your true and proper worship. Do not conform to the pattern of this world, but be transformed by the renewing of your mind. Then you will be able to test and approve what God's will is—his good, pleasing and perfect will.

Teaching Points

1. Our citizenship is in heaven - When in an international environment, one of the first things mentioned while introducing oneself is the country you are from. Paul reminds us that our core identity is as believers. Identifying ourselves as followers of Christ should be second nature. Do your friends and co-workers all know you are a believer? They should.

But this principle has several more implications.

Firstly, we are all foreigners in this world, aliens even! I imagine an alien would be shocked at many things people do on earth, and so should we. As foreigners in this world, we are ambassadors for Christ.

2 Corinthians 5:20 – *We are therefore Christ's ambassadors, as though God were making his appeal through us. We implore you on Christ's behalf: Be reconciled to God.*

An ambassador is, most importantly, a representative of his home country. He represents its culture and values. Beyond this, he seeks to bridge the gap between the two countries.

As ambassadors for Christ, we seek to bring people into peace with Him. We strive to reconcile the world to God by encouraging "immigration" from the kingdom of this world to the kingdom of heaven, made possible by the cross. We also represent Christ. He is the light of the world. And we, too, are lights reflecting His love and holiness to the lost. As foreigners in this world, we should not engage in its sinful practices. Instead, we must be in the world but not of the world.

And as sojourners in this world, we must not get attached to it. We know that the things we see in this world are temporary. But the things of God are eternal.

Secondly, a citizen of a country has certain privileges. As citizens of God's kingdom, He extends to us many privileges that non-citizens do not enjoy.

When I visit American consulates in other countries, I often see very long lines of non-citizens waiting to get access, but citizens can jump the queue and go straight in. It is a privilege to be an American citizen; I get special treatment.

Spiritually, this is true for believers. Here are some of the special privileges God extends to citizens of His kingdom:

- Forgiveness of sins
- Adoption as sons and daughters
- Promise of answered prayer
- Eternal life
- Promise of providence (Romans 8:28)

Application: How can you better represent Christ as His ambassador? In recent years, there have been increasing arguments and divisions online. How can you shine the light of Christ on social media such as Facebook? What is one way you can be in the world but not of the world?

Philippians 4:1-9

Outline

I. Stand firm (1)
II. Encouragement to individual believers to live in harmony (2-3)
III. Rejoice in the Lord and take everything to Him in prayer (4-7)
IV. Meditate on pure things (8-9)

I. Stand firm (1)

Discussion Questions

- What is the "therefore" there for?
- What is Paul's joy and crown?
- What does it mean that the Philippians are his joy and crown?
- In what way are they to stand firm in the Lord?
- Why does it say stand firm "in the Lord" and not just "stand firm?"

Teaching Points

1. Therefore - The instruction in verse 1 to stand firm is linked to the previous passage. That section describes the onward push of the believers' lives, the danger of false teachers, and the knowledge that our citizenship is in heaven. Because of these things, believers are to stand firm in the Lord. Any one of the world, false teachers, or complacency could cause believers to fall away. In other words, standing firm is a key application from what we have learned in chapter three.

2. The two phrases "whom I long to see" and "my joy and my crown" both act as adjectives to describe Paul's brethren, the Philippians. He has already

expressed his hope to see them throughout the book. They are his joy because they are doing well and growing. The fruit Paul sees in their lives encourages him. They are his crown because they are a success of his ministry. He can and did "give them" to God as his work for God, like we will give our crowns to God one day.

3. Stand firm in the Lord - This command is often given in the Word. It shows the solid foundation that we have. Because of our foundation on Christ, we can stand firm. In stark contrast, the one without faith is tossed about by the waves of the sea (James 1:6) and the foolish builder's house on the sand will collapse (Matthew 7:24-27).

4. In this way - Paul says to stand firm "in this way" or in some translations "thus." In what way? By setting their minds on the things above, forgetting the past, and pushing forward to the future to press on for the prize of the upward call. They are to emulate Paul's example in this. This kind of forget yesterday (its hurts, failures, sins, and achievements) and push on toward the future attitude is what allows believers to stand firm in their faith and continue growing day by day.

5. In the Lord - We have no hope to stand firm on our own by sheer willpower. Though a person may be able to give the appearance of following the Lord on the outside by his own strength, if it is not from a reliance on God, it will be short lived. Our only hope for spiritual success is to rely on the Lord.

II. Encouragement to individual believers to live in harmony (2-3)

Discussion Questions

● Who are Euodia and Syntyche?

- Why do you think Paul felt it necessary to specifically encourage them to live in harmony?
- Why say again "in the Lord"? What does this phrase mean?
- Who is the true companion Paul refers to?
- What did Paul want him to do?
- In what way do you think this individual could help Euodia and Syntyche live in harmony?
- What does this personal section show us about our own responsibility in the church?
- Why did Paul often use the term "workers"?
- What does this show us about our responsibility as believers?

Teaching Points

1. Paul encourages two sisters in unity - This is one of only a few cases where Paul singles out individual believers in his letter. It seems clear that he had heard some news (maybe from Epaphroditus) that Euodia and Syntyche were having issues getting along.

For whatever reason, friction or conflict had developed between them and they weren't living in unity. Such kind of factions are so dangerous to a church's well-being that Paul considered it necessary to single them out, exhorting them to resolve the issue before it grew any bigger.

Application: It is all too common for believers to divide and hold grudges against each other. Satan wants to promote disunity. You must be vigilant and work hard to maintain unity (Ephesians 4:1). Part of that is being alert to any issues and then dealing with them quickly. Jesus instructed the people that unity was so important they should even leave their gifts at the altar to seek reconciliation. Is there a brother or sister who has an issue against you or vice-versa? Contact them this week to resolve it and restore your relationship before it gets worse.

2. In the Lord - Here we see this phrase appears again. People have no hope of living in unity without the Lord. We have too many sins, too many differences, and too many different opinions. Yet with the Lord, all things

are possible, and we can truly be one. God's grace is enough to overcome. Ask Him for the love and compassion to forgive those who have hurt you.

Possibly Silas or Barnabus

3. True companion - Some scholars believe that the Greek for this should be translated as a proper name. Either way, Paul is clearly referring to a specific person in the Philippian church. It could be an elder or perhaps someone close to Euodia and Syntyche. His job was to help these women and all the fellow believers to live in harmony.

From this personal reference, we should be reminded that all the principles in the Bible have practical applications. Paul realizes these principles are not just pieces of knowledge to put in our heads, but they are to be applied to everyday life. He didn't hesitate to exhort individuals to apply such principles to their own lives, and he even encouraged others in the church to help the brethren put these principles into action.

Be careful not to focus on doctrine to the exclusion of practical application. Both are important. Without obedience to the Word, knowledge is worthless.

Application: You can be like this "true companion." A true companion is a friend who says what needs to be said to help others grow, even when they may not want to hear it. A true companion comes alongside and spurs his friends to love and do good deeds. Consider how you can encourage your Christian friends to obey the Word. When you do, try to encourage them in specific ways, not just general ways.

4. Workers - Paul often uses this word for believers. He doesn't say fellow "waiters," "watchers," "sitters," or "listeners." It is a subtle reminder that all of us are to be God's workers. Each of us has specific work to do that He has prepared for us.

Application: What work is God calling you to do for Him today?

III. Rejoice in the Lord and take everything to Him in prayer (4-7)

Discussion Questions

- What do you think it means to rejoice? Smile and laugh excitedly?
- When are we to rejoice?
- How can you rejoice even in the midst of trials or disappointments?
- How can we let our gentle spirit be known to all men?
- Is verse 6 a suggestion?
- Is worry something that you can control?
- Why are we not supposed to worry?
- What is one thing that sometimes causes you worry?
- What might be the difference between concern and worry?
- What is worrying good for?
- What does it mean to pray to God "in everything"?
- If God already knows everything that we are thinking and experiencing, why is it important to take everything to Him in prayer?
- Share an example of something you're thankful for.
- What is something about a trial that you are thankful for?
- Why does it say that this peace is beyond understanding?
- Have you ever experienced this kind of peace? When?

Cross-References

Verses on Worry:

Matthew 6:27-30 – Can any one of you by worrying add a single hour to your life?
"And why do you worry about clothes? See how the flowers of the field grow. They do not labor or spin. Yet I tell you that not even Solomon in all his splendor was dressed like one of these.

Proverbs 12:25 – Anxiety weighs down the heart, but a kind word cheers it up.

Matthew 6:25 – Therefore I tell you, do not worry about your life, what you will eat or drink; or about your body, what you will wear. Is not life more than food, and the body more than clothes?

1 Peter 5:7 - Cast all your anxiety on him because he cares for you.

Verses on Joy:

James 1:2-4 – Consider it pure joy, my brothers and sisters, whenever you face trials of many kinds, because you know that the testing of your faith produces perseverance. Let perseverance finish its work so that you may be mature and complete, not lacking anything.

Psalms 40:16 – But may all who seek you rejoice and be glad in you; may those who long for your saving help always say, "The Lord is great!"

Psalms 28:7 – The Lord is my strength and my shield; my heart trusts in him, and he helps me. My heart leaps for joy, and with my song I praise him.

Verses on Thanksgiving:

Psalms 31:19 – How abundant are the good things that you have stored up for those who fear you, that you bestow in the sight of all, on those who take refuge in you.

Psalms 107:1 - Give thanks to the Lord, for he is good; his love endures forever.

Verses on Peace:

Psalms 119:16 – I delight in your decrees; I will not neglect your word.

Isaiah 26:3 – You will keep in perfect peace those whose minds are steadfast, because they trust in you.

Isaiah 54:10 – Though the mountains be shaken and the hills be removed, yet my unfailing love for you will not be shaken nor my covenant of peace be removed," says the Lord, who has compassion on you.

Teaching Points

1. Rejoice in the Lord always -

Philippians 4:4 - Rejoice in the Lord always; again I will say, rejoice.

God commands us to rejoice. It is not a suggestion. And He tells us to do it all the time. By God's grace, it is possible for us to rejoice even in the midst of great trials or difficulties.

In Acts 16, Paul and Silas were thrown into prison. Prisons in those days were dirty and smelly. Their feet were put in stocks. Circumstances were not good. It was a serious trial for them. They were not in prison because of their own sin. Paul and Silas had been faithfully serving God and sharing the good news. And yet God allowed them to be wrongfully taken and thrown in prison. Some people would become bitter and angry and question God, "God, have you abandoned me? I was serving you! How can you let this happen?"

You know the story. Paul and Silas were singing hymns to the Lord in prison. Eventually the jailer and his family were saved. Although they didn't know what it was at the time, God had a clear purpose in allowing this trial to happen. The lesson from Paul and Silas is simple, no matter how bad things get around us, we decide how to respond.

Because God commands you to rejoice, it means that you can choose whether or not you do. In other words, your emotions are under your control. While you will face circumstances outside of your control, you choose how to respond to them.

Joy is a decision.

Habakkuk 3:17-18 - *Though the fig tree does not bud and there are no grapes on the vines, though the olive crop fails and the fields produce no food, though there are no sheep in the pen and no cattle in the stalls, yet I will rejoice in the Lord, I will be joyful in God my Savior.*

Note what Habakkuk says in verse 18, "I WILL rejoice." He makes a decision. He decides in his heart and before the Lord that no matter how difficult things become, he will respond with a good attitude and be joyful. True joy is not an artificial smile that we paste on to cover over our true feelings.

When I went through training for the teaching job I have, my school told all the teachers to "check our problems at the door." In the classroom, we are supposed to smile and pretend to be happy regardless of how we feel. So in the office, teachers might be complaining or upset, but in the classroom, they smile. But real joy is not like this, merely a fake exterior we put up to show others.

Neither does joy mean there is no room for sadness. Rather, we are commanded to "weep with those who weep." There is a time and a place for grieving. Was Habakkuk happy about all of the disasters the Babylonians would wreak on his people and nation? Did he hear about this and say, "Woo hoo!" No. Happiness and joy are different.

Happiness is primarily a feeling that we have which is triggered by exterior things such as the people around us. It is not natural that we would be happy when for example, someone around us dies. And yet, even in those situations, we can make a decision that we will not complain. We will not become bitter and angry toward God. We will not become grumpy and upset with the people around us.

Joy is a decision that, from our heart, we will keep a good attitude before the Lord and men. We will remain thankful and optimistic. We will remember God's goodness and place our faith in the fact that the trial we face has a purpose.

Joy comes from the Lord. The closer our relationship to Him, the easier it will be to "rejoice always."

Application: Perhaps you have not responded well to the trials in your life. Perhaps you have complained. Perhaps you have become short-tempered and easily irritated. Perhaps you have even allowed anger toward the Lord to build up in your hearts. Will you decide today to be joyful even amid difficulties?

2. The Lord is near -

- He is near because He is omnipresent.
- He is near because He is omniscient.
- He is near because He didn't leave the world to go its own way after creation.
- He is near because He cares for us.
- He is near because He will come again soon.

3. Do not be anxious about anything - Here is another command. Simply put, do not worry. Wow, that is a difficult one! Since God commands us not to worry, it means that worrying is a sin. Why?

At its heart, worrying demonstrates a lack of faith (Matthew 6:30). It could be a lack of faith in God's ability to take care of your needs, or it could be a lack of faith in His goodness, believing that He wants what is best for you.

Worrying accomplishes nothing. It can cause you to lose sleep, become depressed, perform poorly, grow ulcers, and cause other health and mental problems.

1 Peter 5:7 tells you that *"God cares for you."*

Think about that thought for a minute. The Creator of the universe, King of Kings, and Lord of Lords cares deeply about you as an individual. He showed it through Christ's death on the cross. God is not an impersonal force. He is not a distant observer. He is watching you closely. He has a plan for you. He wants the very best for you, just like a loving parent wants the best for the kid. But the parent may not always know what is best for their kid. Even if they do, they may not have the power to see it happen. But God knows what is best for us, AND He can make it happen. That is a good friend to have on our side!

The Bible is filled with commands not to do something, and many of those are followed by commands of what to do instead. This verse is no different. Believers are not to just sit around telling themselves, "Don't worry. Don't worry. Don't worry."

4. Don't worry. Pray. - Instead of worrying, we are to proactively take our concerns to God and ask for His help. Paul says that we are to pray to God "in everything." The attitude reflected here is a lifestyle of prayer. Nothing is too big or too small to pray about. You should pray to God about your work, your family, decisions you make, character, health, church, missions, hobbies, etc.

In some ways, worry is almost the opposite of prayer. Great men and women of faith in the Bible were prayer warriors, bringing their petitions into the presence of God.

Application: We all know this verse already. The idea is simple. Pray. How can you develop a lifestyle of prayer? What is one way you can practice the principle of praying to God about "everything?" This week, intentionally pray more, not just at meal-times or before sleep or after church. Pray throughout each day. Talk to God about how you are feeling and what you are struggling with. Ask Him for wisdom. Praise Him when you are reminded of His glory. Your prayers don't have to be long. But by praying throughout the day, you will be able to keep your focus on the Lord instead of your circumstances.

5. With thanksgiving: Also a command. Our prayers are to be filled with thanksgiving, not only when we get something we want but when we get

something we don't want.

Do you remember when you were a kid and received a gift of socks or perhaps a sweater for Christmas? It may have been difficult to be thankful when you were hoping for the new latest and greatest gadget. But your parents probably trained you to be thankful anyway. And though you may not have realized it at the time, you needed those clothes. They were boring but necessary.

Similarly, God wants us to be thankful in everything. Often times in our limited wisdom, we do not recognize the "why" of what God allows to happen in our lives. Why do I feel such pain? Why did God allow me to be so hurt?

But we need to recognize the "who." The who is God. He allowed these things to happen for our good.

Romans 8:28 - *And we know that in all things God works for the good of those who love him, who have been called according to his purpose.*

When you truly believe this verse, you will be able to genuinely thank God even in the midst of life's greatest trials.

Application: What is one difficult thing in your life that you need to decide to be thankful for?

6. He will give you peace - This peace cannot be understood by those who don't understand God. They only know what they can see and feel, but this peace flows from our faith in God and the knowledge that He is sovereign and a good God who watches over us.

This peace protects us. It protects us from rash actions, from complaining, from fear, from anxiety, and from a lack of joy. It protects us from sinning.

Question for group sharing: When is one time you have experienced this profound peace from God?

IV. Meditate on pure things (8-9)

Discussion Questions

- What does it mean to dwell on these things?
- Why are we to dwell on these things?
- How might this affect our joy and thanksgiving?
- What kind of specific things can you think of that fit into this category?
- What are some examples of unhealthy things we shouldn't spend time thinking about?
- Why does Paul give himself as an example to follow? Isn't Christ our only example?

Teaching Points

1. Direct your thoughts and don't let them direct you - This passage tells believers we are to control the direction of our thoughts and not be controlled by them. You decide what you think; don't just allow any thought to pop into your head and take over.

How is this possible? What should we do when temptations, worries, and negative thoughts (like gossip or judgmental attitudes, boasting or pride) pop into our heads?

We are to meditate on positive things that will enrich our spirit instead of tempting us.

Proverbs 4:23 - *Watch over your heart with all diligence, For from it flow the springs of life.*

It is important to pay attention to what goes into your mind. What goes in will affect you.

Bull moose battle each fall during mating season for supremacy. The toughest bull that wins the fights will get the girl. These magnificent beasts go head-to-head, smashing each other will tremendous impact. Their antlers are their weapons, and often they lose the fight because they are broken. The strongest animal with the toughest antlers wins. Although the battle appears to be fought in the fall, it is actually fought in spring. Whichever moose has the best diet and receives the best nourishment in the spring will win the fight in the fall.

Our spiritual battle against temptation is also like that. When you nourish your mind with positive spiritual food, you will think about these things, and you will be less susceptible to temptation. The new you will grow stronger, while the fleshly you will grow weaker.

On the other hand, if you feed your mind spiritual junk food, then you will think about these things and be more susceptible to temptation. The fleshly you will grow stronger, while the new you will grow weaker.

Some positive things to meditate on include Bible verses, Christian songs, Christian biographies, or God's character. Other examples are testimonies of other believers, things God has done in our lives, or things to be thankful for.

Some negative things include gossip, scandals, celebrity news, immoral movies or novels, worry, and pornography.

The world finds sins and scandals fascinating, but deeds worthy of praise are often not nearly as popular.

Question for consideration: Why do gossip and scandals attract such attention compared to noble things worthy of meditation?

Philippians 4:10-23

Outline

I. The Philippians helped Paul financially (10)
II. Paul had learned to be content in all situations through Christ (11-13)
III. The Philippians generously supported Paul (14-19)
IV. Benediction and greetings (20-23)

I. The Philippians helped Paul financially (10)

Discussion Questions

- Why was Paul rejoicing?
- What does he mean that they had revived their concern for him?
- Why had there been a lull in their giving to Paul?
- Is that a good reason not to give?

Teaching Points

1. Paul was rejoicing - Paul's joy was not because of the money he going to receive from them. He was happy to see them doing well, to see them willing to share.

My two-year-old daughter has a comfort blanket. She doesn't want to sleep without it. It is her most cherished possession. It, therefore, brought a smile to my face when she offered to share this blanket with me and even pointed out her favorite corner that I, too, could suck. I was not joyful because I longed for the blanket, but because it was encouraging to see her so willing to share!

Likewise, Paul was joyful to hear that the Philippians were willing to share with him what God had blessed them with.

2. You have revived your concern for me - The Philippians had given financial help to Paul before, about ten years prior, when he was in Thessalonica (15-16). Now they once again wanted to help.

Paul says that they had not given in the interim because they did not have the "opportunity." It could be that Paul did not go near their region again, or it could be that they were unable to offer more support due to other financial reasons.

II. Paul had learned to be content in all situations through Christ (11-13)

Discussion Questions

- What was Paul's motivation for bringing this up with them?
- Are you content?
- Can you give any example where perhaps you were recently, or any time you can remember, not content? What caused this?
- Was Paul content because circumstances were favorable? What kind of unfavorable circumstances did he endure?
- What is the root cause of discontent? What are opposites of contentment (envy, coveting, complaining, etc.)?
- Does Paul teach that having a lot is not good?
- What was the "secret" of Paul's contentment?
- What is the world's solution when they are discontent? What are common areas of discontent?
- Verse 13 is often pulled out of context as a sort of super-man verse, telling Christians we can do anything. Looking at it in context, what can we learn about what Paul is really saying here?

- Can you think of any examples in the Bible of believers who lacked what they needed, and God provided for them? (Israel in the wilderness, Elijah…)

Cross-References

Verses on Contentment:

Psalms 37:16 - Better the little that the righteous have than the wealth of many wicked.

1 Timothy 6:6, 8 - But godliness with contentment is great gain. But if we have food and clothing, we will be content with that.

Hebrews 13:5 - Keep your lives free from the love of money and be content with what you have, because God has said, "Never will I leave you; never will I forsake you."

Ecclesiastes 5:10 - Whoever loves money never has enough; whoever loves wealth is never satisfied with their income. This too is meaningless.

Luke 12:15 - Then he said to them, "Watch out! Be on your guard against all kinds of greed; life does not consist in an abundance of possessions."

Teaching Points

1. Paul had learned how to be content - Paul had many experiences in his life of service to Christ, most of them difficult. Shipwrecks, imprisonments, scourging, stoning, beating, and many more hardships were routine. So, it could be said that his circumstances taught him how to be content.

But this would not accurately show the whole picture because many people go through hardships and yet never learn how to be content. A more accurate statement is that God used the trials Paul faced to teach him about contentment. Yet Paul still had to learn this lesson.

What is the secret of contentment?

Paul already told us of his mindset in following after Christ.

Philippians 3:7-9 - *But whatever were gains to me I now consider loss for the sake of Christ. What is more, I consider everything a loss because of the surpassing worth of knowing Christ Jesus my Lord, for whose sake I have lost all things. I consider them garbage, that I may gain Christ and be found in him, not having a righteousness of my own that comes from the law, but that which is through faith in Christ—the righteousness that comes from God on the basis of faith.*

He counted all the things in this world as rubbish and set his heart completely on pursuing Christ. That is the key to contentment.

There are two possible outcomes when a person sets his heart on things in this world:

A. He gets what he wants. But then he finds out that it cannot make him happy and is therefore discontent. If a person chases after marriage, money, achievement, or fame (or any other thing in this world), he will find that it cannot satisfy him.

B. He doesn't get what he wants. And then he is discontent because he doesn't get what he hoped for.

Psalm 37:4 - *Delight yourself in the LORD, and he will give you the desires of your heart.*

Contentment does not depend on circumstances. It is a mindset. It comes from a relationship with and a reliance upon God. It is possible to be content, and even joyful in every circumstance (Habakkuk 3:17-19).

Application: Are you generally content? Is there something which you want but don't have, which you are unhappy about? Spend some time in prayer and tell God that He is enough for you. Ask Him to satisfy you and change the desires of your heart to match His.

87

2. I can do all things through Christ who strengthens me - Philippians 4:13 is a great verse, but it is also frequently taken out of context. Verse cards often feature this verse, and many people memorize it, claiming the statement that they can do anything by God's strength. It is not hard to see how this could give the wrong impression.

Free climbers could claim this verse and climb dangerous cliffs with no ropes because they can do "all things."

A bank robber could claim this statement as God's guarantee of success.

These extreme examples show us that clearly, it doesn't mean anything. One condition is that these things are enabled by God, who gives strength. And since God would not enable sin, any foolish, reckless, or sinful action is not in line with this promise.

That is obvious. But Christians may also try to claim this promise for doing many other good things, which are also not covered by this statement. One important rule when interpreting Scripture is to pay attention to the context. The context quantifies the statement in verse 13.

What is the context?

It is learning to be content. Paying attention to the context it shows us that verse 13 means, "I can be content in any situation through him who strengthens me."

The contentment does not come from his own willpower but from trust in God. God is the one who gives the strength to respond to trials with a steadfast, joyful contentment.

III. The Philippians generously supported Paul (14-19)

Discussion Questions

- In what way did the Philippians share with Paul in his affliction?
- What distinction did the Philippians have in verse 15? What does this tell us about them?
- How many times had they given to Paul? Why? Shouldn't Paul make money on his own?
- Why was Paul so happy about their generosity?
- How did their generosity profit them?
- Does God also want us to give today?
- To whom or what? Why? When? How much?
- What are the most common reasons for not giving?
- Are these good reasons?
- What about if we are on a very tight budget?

Cross References

Verses on Generosity:

Proverbs 22:9 - The generous will themselves be blessed, for they share their food with the poor.

Matthew 6:3-4 - But when you give to the needy, do not let your left hand know what your right hand is doing, so that your giving may be in secret. Then your Father, who sees what is done in secret, will reward you.
Luke 6:38 - Give, and it will be given to you. A good measure, pressed down, shaken together and running over, will be poured into your lap. For with the measure you use, it will be measured to you."

Romans 8:32 - He who did not spare his own Son, but gave him up for us all—how will he not also, along with him, graciously give us all things?

Acts 20:35 - In everything I did, I showed you that by this kind of hard work we must help the weak, remembering the words the Lord Jesus himself said: 'It is more blessed to give than to receive.'"

1 Timothy 6:18 - Command them to do good, to be rich in good deeds, and to be generous and willing to share.

2 Corinthians 9:7 - Each of you should give what you have decided in your heart to give, not reluctantly or under compulsion, for God loves a cheerful giver.

Teaching Points

1. It was kind of you to share my trouble - Paul does not seek to minimize their contributions by talking about contentment. He simply wants the focus to be on God. We can simultaneously hold to both the truth that God is good and wants us to be content in all situations and the truth that believers should generously support God's workers.

2. No churches gave to me except you - It is a sad statement. Paul was appointed by Christ to take the gospel to the Gentiles. He established churches, made disciples, trained leaders, and penned Scripture. It could accurately be said that, with exception of Jesus, no individual had more influence on the church than Paul.

And yet, there were long periods of time in his ministry when churches did not support him. Certainly, Paul's own ministry philosophy contributed partially to this. He very seldom asked for support, instead choosing to work himself so as not to burden the churches (2 Corinthians 9). In addition, he did not want to be accused of greed.

But even so, churches should have been more zealous (like the Philippians) to take the initiative to try to support Paul than they were.

Many modern-day churches would do well to learn from the example of the Philippians. A very substantial portion of every church's budget should go to missions, outreach, and discipleship. But many churches focus on facilities, buildings, robes, and programs instead of supporting those who are advancing the gospel. A percentage cannot be placed on it, but the church's priority should be on missions.

Application: Consider how you can be an influence in your church to support missions. Perhaps you can recommend a specific person or ministry to support. You can be a voice to encourage your church to be outward focused.

3. I seek the fruit that increases to you - Paul clearly states that his pleasure in this comes from his knowledge that it is good for them to be so generous.

Note that we should not go around begging for money and saying, "I just want to bless you by taking your money!" Unscrupulous televangelists may do this. Becoming rich, they purchase more private jets and up their already luxuriant lifestyle. All the while, they say, "I don't want to deny their gifts and therefore deny them a blessing."

4. Verse 18 - A generous gift is a "sacrifice acceptable and pleasing to God." When we show love by supporting God's workers, we show love to God Himself. In the Old Testament, the Israelites gave to the priests and Levites as a way to give tithes and offerings to God.

Today we give to missionaries, Bible teachers, church planters, evangelists, and disciple-makers.

Application: Take some time to evaluate your own giving. Are you being generous? Prayerfully consider if God would have you add to your regular giving. Consider where your money would go the farthest to fulfilling the Great Commission. And practice sacrificial giving, which will be pleasing to God.

5. My God will richly supply every need of yours - A generous person does not need to fear the future. This verse applies not only to the Philippians but to all believers who generously support God's work. God will richly take care of the needs of the generous.

Note that this is not a promise of prosperity. It does not say, "if you give X amount, then God will give you back X amount more." It does not say that God will give you what you want. And it does not say that God will make you rich. It simply says that God will take care of your needs.

When the Shunammite woman gave her last bit of food to Elisha, God took care of her and her family. She didn't become rich. But she had enough to eat.

God is rich, and He delights in giving good gifts to His children. In the Old Testament, Israelites were to give the "first fruits" of their crops. It meant giving the best to God, but it also meant giving first before they forgot or used it all up. They gave to God first because it was a priority.

Some people are worried to do this because they are scared that they will not have enough. Stop worrying. Trust God. He will take care of you.

IV. Benediction and greetings (20-23)

Discussion Questions

- How does Paul end this book?
- What lessons can we learn from his conclusion?

Teaching Points

1. Benediction - Paul ends with a benediction. He gives all the glory to God. It is a good way to end! The ending is a reminder that everything Paul said was from God and for His glory, and the purpose of all of his instruction to them was so that they could glorify God more.

2. Greetings - Paul ends with greetings. His letters often end in this way. Chances to see each other were few and far between in the ancient world. Distances were long, and roads were not good. It, therefore, was natural to

add on greetings in his letters as a brief way to show love and concern among the brethren.

Interestingly, he mentions the saints in "Caesar's household." Remember that Paul was under house arrest in Rome. While there he actively shared the gospel. And it was making an impact! Even members of Caesar's own household had come to Christ right under his nose! This simple statement is a reminder that all things (even Paul's imprisonment) work together for good to those who love God and are called according to His purpose (Romans 8:28).

Final Note: You can view more studies like this on over 30 books of the Bible at our website at studyandobey.com.

Made in the USA
Coppell, TX
14 February 2023